Little Next Step

How to Be a Little Sod. Book 2

Simon Brett, closely acquainted with the charms of parenthood, is the ideal interlocutor for this infant Pepys. Himself a noted diarist (compiler of *The Faber Book of Diaries* and of Radio 4's *Dear Diary*), he is also well known as a humorist, writer and frequent broadcaster. Simon Brett lives in Sussex with his wife and family.

Tony Ross is one of Britain's leading illustrators of children's books, and has won many awards both nationally and internationally. He lives in Cheshire with his wife.

And don't miss the first volume of the Little Sod's diaries

HOW TO BE A LITTLE SOD

by Simon Brett, illustrated by Tony Ross

Also available in paperback £3.99

Simon Brett

Little Sod's Next Step

How to Be a Little Sod. Book 2

illustrated by
Tony Ross

VISTA

TO HAL MOTLEY
(who will find nothing in here
that he doesn't know already)

First published in Great Britain 1994
as *Look Who's Walking: Further Diaries of a Little Sod*
by Victor Gollancz

This Vista edition published 1996
Vista is an imprint of the Cassell Group
Wellington House, 125 Strand, London WC2R 0BB

Text copyright © 1994 Simon Brett
Illustrations copyright © 1994 Tony Ross

The right of Simon Brett to be identified as author of this
work and of Tony Ross to be identified as author of the
illustrations has been asserted by them in accordance with
the Copyright, Designs and Patents Act, 1988.

A catalogue record for this book is
available from the British Library.

ISBN 0 575 60133 7

Printed and bound in Great Britain by
Cox & Wyman Ltd, Reading, Berks

96 97 98 99   10 9 8 7 6 5 4 3 2 1

Introduction

For those of you unfamiliar with the first volume of my bestselling memoirs, *How to be a Little Sod* (and there can't be many of you around), here is a brief recap of that momentous first year.

After a rather traumatic entry into the world (not an experience I'd care to repeat) my development was quite astonishing. I increased in weight, went on to solids, mastered sitting up (and falling over), moving around, even said my first word . . . The list is endless and the opportunities for creating mayhem infinite.

And during that first year my parents also developed. Their progress was not as astonishing as mine, but it was still pretty impressive.

Yes, when I think back, they really have come a long way. In the early months they suffered from all kinds of naive illusions. For a start, they thought that having a baby – i.e. me – would not make much difference to their lives. Well, I soon disabused them of that little notion.

They also thought – it almost brings tears to the eyes – that they would be able to go on living selfishly for their own enjoyment. They innocently assumed that they'd have as active a social life after my arrival as they'd had before. They fondly imagined that they'd be able to have just as uninhibited a sex life . . . Ho Hum.

Needless, to say, they were not allowed to suffer these delusions for long. I saw to that.

And, inevitably, it wasn't all plain sailing. At times my parents were painfully slow to learn the appropriate behaviour for people in their position. They even pretended – on occasion – that they had some power over me . . . laughable.

Still, I persevered; it was hard work and it needed a lot of patience, but by the end of the year my parents were as docile as anyone could wish. They fully accepted that only one person called the shots in our household, and that was ME.

So I embark on my second year with confidence, but with some caution. Parents mean well, but you have to keep an eye on them at all times. The moment your back's turned, they're quite capable of trying something on, and so I'm always having to come down on them like a ton of bricks. I'm sorry, but when you're dealing with parents, you have to be cruel to be kind.

But for you, dear reader, what I am offering is pure pleasure. You are uniquely privileged to be able to read selected extracts from the diary of the second year of my life. Lucky you!

Little Sod (me)

Thirteenth Month

DAY 1

Well, here we are – the beginning of my second year.

And how did my parents celebrate the occasion? By being deeply hungover from last night. Typical. When will those two grow up?

I decided to celebrate the occasion by producing my second word. And I knew exactly what that word would be. It was going to be a good one: pithy, to the point, and entirely in character.

The ideal moment to launch the new word came while I was having my bath. She, more or less recovered from Her hangover, was asking yet another of the stupid questions that continually pepper Her dialogue. 'Now does oo want to have oo's hair washed then?' She asked.

I left Her in no doubt about my feelings on the subject.

'NO!' I bawled.

DAY 4

Today, when He came home from work, She tried to get me to reproduce my new word for His benefit. She lifted me on to Her knee and cooed, 'Does oo want to tell oo's Daddy oo's new word then?'

'NO!' I bawled.

I'm sorry to say they were delighted.

DAY 5

I am under a great deal of pressure from Her to 'mix with other children'. She keeps talking about something called a 'Parent and Toddler Group'.

Sounds ghastly to me. From what I've seen of other children, they're self-centred, petulant, uncommunicative Little Sods whose sole aim is to get their own way.

Only room for one of those round here, I'd say.

DAY 6

Another outing for the new word today. His mother came round. 'Does oo love oo's Grandma then?' my mother cooed.

'NO!' I bawled.

NO.

She was terribly apologetic to Her mother-in-law about this, but secretly I think She was delighted. Anyway, She gave me an extra helping of ice cream for tea.

DAY 7

Her mother came round today. 'Does oo hate oo's Granny then?' my mother cooed.

'NO!' I bawled, and they both burst out laughing.

I was disgusted at having been the victim of such a low trick. But I got my own back. Moments later, off Her guard, She said, 'But oo loves oo's Mummy, doesn't oo?'

'NO!' I bawled.

DAY 8

Having made such a big stride forward on the linguistic front, maybe I should concentrate on movement for a while. Just think how much being able to walk will increase my potential for destruction!

DAY 11

Still keen to develop this doomed idea of a Parent and Toddler Group, She asked another mother to bring her child round this morning. I did not care for it.

What's more, the little smartypants could walk, which made me care for it even less.

DAY 12

I'm sure walking can't be that difficult. I mean, it's just a matter of putting one foot in front of the other, isn't it? My parents can do it, after all, and, on the evidence I've seen, I wouldn't describe them as particularly gifted.

I must make a few cautious experiments while they're not watching.

DAY 13

My basic method of locomotion at the moment is crawling, but that does have its limitations. They've worked out my height-range, you see, and just about everything desirable – the CD player, His razor, the electric kettle – is out of my reach. Walking cannot be put off much longer. It's essential for the next stage of my progress in domestic demolition.

DAY 14

At the moment I can stay upright so long as I'm hanging on to something. I feel fairly secure doing that, until my knees start to go. When that happens, I just grip incredibly tight on to whatever I'm holding and sink downwards with my full weight.

This exercise does sometimes have rewarding results. For instance, this morning when She was trying to impress one of Her career friends with how cool and together She was in spite of me, I managed to pull Her skirt off.

DAY 15

She had the mother with that child around again this morning. I'd hardly call two parents and toddlers a 'Group'. All I know is that, as far as I'm concerned, it's at least one toddler too many.

As soon as the child was placed on the floor, I crawled straight towards it.

'Oh look,' She cooed to its mother, 'aren't they pleased to see each other?'

I poked my finger in Smartypants' eye.

DAY 16

While She was in the kitchen this morning doing the ironing, I had a go at standing on my own. I pulled myself up on the arm of the sofa (leaving a very satisfactory smear – you just can't beat a good half-chewed chocolate biscuit). Then I moved as far away as I dared, and let go.

For a brief, dizzying moment, I felt the sensation of standing on my own two feet. All at once my legs buckled, and I landed with a crash on my bottom.

Early days, but I'm getting there.

DAY 18

She took me to the supermarket today. I quite enjoy this, because I'm put in the special sitting bit of the trolley and get whizzed about along the aisles. Dead good – makes me feel like royalty in a carriage. I've even got quite expert at waving in a regal manner to all the surrounding riff-raff.

She is very amused by this little trick and keeps saying how clever I am. Only today did I realize why this is.

She encourages me to wave because it stops me from doing all the other things I usually get up to in a supermarket trolley. What a fool I've been not to notice this earlier.

Made up for lost time. Discovered that by reaching out and grabbing hold of something while being propelled at high speed, I can achieve the supermarket trolley equivalent of a handbrake turn.

She was totally thrown first time I did it. We'd got up quite a head of steam when suddenly I grabbed hold of a shelf at the end of an aisle. The trolley slewed sideways, nearly wrenching Her arms out of their sockets.

As She struggled to regain control, I equally suddenly released my hold. Our vehicle shot off diagonally and cannoned against the trolley of a senior citizen, who was sent sprawling into a display of Special Offer dog food.

This is FUN!

DAY 19

She left me naked for a moment in the bathroom in the middle of a nappy change this morning, and I thought I'd have another go at this standing-on-my-own-two-feet lark.

It was a long time before I fell, but the inevitable could not be held off for ever. As usual, I wobbled, my legs gave out and without my nappy as a cushion, my backside took the full impact.

And this time it *hurt*. Really hurt. I hadn't quite realized the vulnerability of a nappyless bum.

I let out a huge bellow and She came rushing in to comfort me.

My bottom was still red and smarting at bedtime. I think I may put off further experiments in standing up for a while.

DAY 23

Back to the supermarket. She was wary this time and pushed the trolley right down the middle of the aisles so that I couldn't grab anything. I concentrated on the stuff in the trolley instead. Decided to eat it. Some of the packaging must have been designed by Securicor, but I made inroads.

I ate three buns, a chunk of Edam, a banana, half a packet of spaghetti, a sachet of shampoo, a lump of butter and a box of the cat's Munchies.

When I say 'ate', of course I don't mean ate properly – I just sort of chewed and slobbered over everything until it looked absolutely disgusting. Except the Munchies. I ate them. I don't know if you've tried them. They are delicious.

DAY 27

You know, you can't leave a parent alone for a moment. As soon as my back's turned, She starts getting all kinds of ridiculous ideas.

You'll never believe what She started talking about again tonight. It was after my supper and bath, He was home knocking back the Scotch as usual, and I was having my customary before-bed breastfeed.

This is a very comforting routine we've slipped into. She doesn't breastfeed me at any other time. Oh no, I knock back solids with gusto at all other meals. But come the evening, there's nothing nicer than a warm milky drink.

Anyway, after a few satisfying sucks and nibbles, I nodded off, as I often do round that time. I wasn't quite asleep, but it was clear they thought I was.

She started the conversation. 'I rang my boss today. He's very keen for me to get back to work as soon as possible.'

I was thunderstruck. I thought I'd put a firm stop to all that leading-Her-own-life nonsense.

'Good,' He said. 'We could certainly do with the extra money. How soon is "as soon as possible"?'

'As soon as I can get someone sorted out to look after this.'

The very words were heresy. And I particularly dislike being referred to as 'this'.

'You don't think Old Droopy-Drawers'll mind?'

It took me a moment or two to realize that by 'Droopy-Drawers' He meant ME! I can't deny that it cut me to the quick. Nobody looks their best encased in nappies and plastic pants. I'd like to see what kind of a figure He'd cut at the office if he had to wear that lot under his trousers.

'No,' She said angrily. 'Of course not.'

'So you won't have any problem with the weaning?' He asked.

'Virtually *is* weaned,' She replied airily. 'This feed's just for comfort. I'll drop it soon.'

I was appalled by her callousness. I felt betrayed. Here I'd been getting on with my own life, wolfing down my solids and so on, while all the time She had been scheming to get me weaned so She could go and have fun in Her office.

I made sure they suffered for their temerity. Woke up instantly, before any more treason could be uttered, and kept them awake by bawling all night.

Nobody crosses *me* and gets away with it.

DAY 30

Saturday. He took me shopping today, and I think it was my proudest moment yet. As well as all the usual boring stuff, He bought Himself a bottle of whisky in the off-licence section.

Oh, the delicacy with which I waited until His back was turned, neatly lifted the bottle by its neck, let it dangle over the side of the trolley until He turned back and saw it, and, before He had time to do anything, dropped it on to the floor, where it exploded with an extremely satisfying crash.

I don't think I've ever witnessed such a tragic expression on a human face.

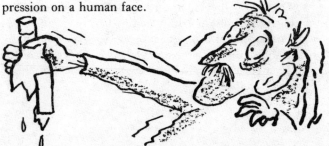

Fourteenth Month

DAY 1

I don't know – no sooner do I get rid of Smartypants when She invites another future Einstein to the house. I've never seen this one before. She met the mother when She was in the hospital having me. Of course, at the time the Other Baby was hardly noticed, being unbelievably less beautiful, talented, advanced, intelligent and generally gorgeous than I was.

But over the last year the Other Baby has been mentioned with increasing and rather alarming frequency. According to Her, this miniature Einstein has had the nerve to make certain developmental advances quicker than I have. And She is starting to go on about it.

I must monitor this tendency with great attention, or I could have problems later on. If I'm not careful, this Other Baby will grow up to be the bane of my life – you know the sort of thing: beating Boris Spassky before it cuts all its teeth, winning an Oscar for its perfect recital of 'Humpty Dumpty' and having an exhibition of fingerpainting at the Tate.

DAY 7

Baby Einstein cropped up in conversation again today. Apparently not only does the little bugger have a vocabulary of twenty words, it's also been walking for the past two months! Well, it *would*, wouldn't it?

My reaction to this is obvious – nobody likes a smartarse.

Hm . . . Maybe I should revise my proposed schedule for this Taking the First Step business.

DAY 8

Still undecided about the First Step. There could be disadvantages. For instance, walking too soon could result in my being picked up less often. At the moment I keep being scooped up and carried around in style. I don't want to give that up in too much of a hurry.

And I know them. After the initial excitement and cooing over my First Step, they'll start taking it for granted. Before I know where I am, they'll be expecting me to walk *everywhere*.

DAY 11

Did a good tease today. They were both there and I had pulled myself up on the arm of His armchair. I moved away a bit, so I was just supporting myself on one hand.

They got very excited by this. He even started watching me instead of the telly. So, given my audience's full attention, I played up to it. I lifted one foot off the ground and pointed it forward, poised like a ballet dancer.

'Look,' She hissed. 'Look! I think this is it . . . Baby's First Step.'

I milked the situation for as long as I could. Kept unscrunching my hand as if I was about to let go of the armchair, and waving my foot in the air as if about to launch myself forward.

After a couple of minutes, though, I began to get uncomfortable, so, with a little sigh, I subsided grace-fully back on to my bottom.

The disappointment on their faces was pitiful to see. And yes, that bloody Baby Einstein got mentioned again. Looks like one small step from him represents one giant leap forward for them . . .

DAY 12

I decided that a little cautious experimentation was in order. I waited till She was safely occupied in the kitchen folding up the washing (since I have at least three changes of clothes a day, that usually keeps her going for ages). I crawled into the sitting room and pulled myself up against a chair. Then I got into the same position as yesterday – holding on with one hand with one leg up in the air. I expect Nureyev started in much the same way.

I glanced at the door to check She was still out of the way, then looked round the room to find a suitable objective for my First Walk. (I'd decided I wasn't going to bother with the First Step stage. I know the basic principle involved. After you've done the one step it's simply a matter of doing the same thing again and again. Don't know why everyone makes so much fuss about it.)

I reckoned the table was about the right distance away. Only a few steps. Easy-peasy.

Nonchalantly, and in one graceful movement, I directed my free leg forward and propelled myself away from the chair.

For a moment I hung in space, then found myself going into an uncontrolled spin. The room swirled around me. The floor came up to meet me with sickening speed.

Hm. I'm obviously missing something in this walking business. Shame it's not a bruised bum.

DAY 13

I've decided to jack in the 'do-it-yourself' method for the moment because they've bought me a Babywalker. This is a circular thing on wheels into which a baby is placed, so that its feet touch the ground and it can propel itself around.

It's going to be terrific fun. I really fancy zooming round the house like an avenging Dalek – pity it can't go upstairs.

EXTERMINATE

DAY 15

A friend of Hers came round today and brought me a present. It was a little brightly coloured plastic table with holes in it through which little brightly coloured plastic rods can be banged with a little brightly coloured plastic hammer. On the box I noted the word 'Educational'. That really is the Kiss of Death.

There was only one thing to do. I ignored the thing completely.

Then they both got down on the floor and started showing me how it worked. 'Look, hammer, hammer, hammer!' they said. 'And look – when we hammer, the little rods go *down*, don't they?'

Well, of course they do, but what's the point? So you hammer them all down and what you've got is a brightly coloured plastic table with a lot of brightly coloured plastic rods sticking out the bottom . . . does this really advance the cause of human knowledge in any useful direction?

'And then look – *you turn it over!*' they announced gleefully. 'And then what do you do? Yes – hammer, hammer, hammer – and the little rods go *down* again, don't they?'

Is it any wonder that the academic standards in this country have dropped?

DAY 17

I'm really getting the hang of this Babywalker thing. Don't have much control over steering it yet, but I'm chipping great chunks of paint off the skirting boards.

DAY 18

The cat didn't realize this morning how much more mobile I could be in the Babywalker.

Mind you, it did by the afternoon.

Eventually, after some hours of being cornered and persecuted, it escaped. The boom of the slamming cat-flap reverberated through the house.

Cat hadn't come back by the time I was put to bed.

DAY 19

Cat not back yet.

You know, She's serious about this going back to work business. She has actually set up interviews with three potential candidates for the job of looking after me. (They have decided against a nanny – too expensive – or an au pair – too inexperienced – and agreed to go for a good old-fashioned 'Mother's Help'.) The first applicant came today.

From my point of view, they are all bound to be extremely unsuitable, but since I can't say anything, I have to try to make *me* seem unsuitable to *them*.

With this first one I crossed my eyes, drooled and made alarming little grunting noises.

For a moment I thought I'd ruined my own cause when the candidate announced that she was trained to look after children with special learning difficulties. Luckily, my mum was so offended by the idea there was anything wrong with me that She sent the girl packing.

One down. Can I get rid of the other two so easily?

DAY 20

The second applicant came today. I threw up over her (none of that projectile vomiting practice in my first year was wasted, you know).

This one, who incidentally was built like a Sumo wrestler, laughed heartily and said she'd soon cure me of *that* little habit. As she did so, she gave me a look that would have frozen the blood of a lesser child, which seemed to say, 'Just wait till I get you on your own – then we'll see who's boss.' I returned the challenge with matching venom.

DAY 22

Third candidate came today. As she leant forward to pat me (I'm not a dog, for heaven's sake), I bit her on the finger. The girl, who was only about twenty and dishy with it, laughed heartily and said I was just showing off how many teeth I'd got.

So then I smashed into her in my Babywalker and laddered her tights.

I regret to say that my tactics didn't have the desired deterrent effect. I would have thought that, as a job, looking after me was marginally less attractive than modelling kebab skewers, but this candidate – and the other girl – seemed dead keen on the idea. I didn't know the employment situation was quite so desperate.

I decided, if I'd got to have either of them, I'd rather have the dishy one. Anything would be preferable to being left alone with Michelin Man's mother.

At the end of both interviews my mother was all businesslike and professional, saying She'd let them know Her decision after She'd spoken to Her husband.

She made it sound as if this meant She'd consult Him about the choice, though I knew full well it just meant She'd tell him what She'd decided.

I also knew there was no way She'd let the young dishy one anywhere near Him.

Oh dear. I know who I'm going to end up with . . .

DAY 23

Yes. The brick-built Sumo wrestler it is. I heard my mother phoning her to pass on the glad tidings.

Apparently she's called Beth – though I bet in the ring she's known under some nickname. What is the Japanese for 'Heavy Goods Vehicle'? I shall christen her 'the Juggernaut'.

I mustered all my skills to avert the awful fate that is being lined up for me.

I was very clingy all day and kept grabbing at Her breasts as if I wanted feeding. With great difficulty I managed to eat little if any of my solid food and, come the before-bed feed, latched on to Her like a sink-plunger.

If I stimulate the milk production enough, maybe I can reverse this weaning process . . . ?

She is utterly unfeeling. When they were going down-stairs after putting me in my cot this evening, I heard Her saying to Him, 'Baby's only playing up because of the Mother's Help; has somehow caught on to the idea that things are about to change and is kicking up a stink because of it.'

'Don't let it get to you,' He said.

'Oh, I won't,' She replied blithely.

I let out a bellow as if I'd suddenly been impaled by a falling church steeple.

It worked. There was doubt in Her voice as She said, 'Maybe there really is something wrong . . . ?'

'Just trying it on,' He reassured Her. 'Knows that sort of crying gets to you every time.'

'Well, it does. Maybe I should go back and—'

'No, you come down and have a drink. Baby'll soon get bored and stop.'

She was still unsure. 'Well . . .'

I let out another stop-stop-I'm-being-disembowelled bellow to make her feel really rotten.

And do you know what He said? 'This'll all be much better when you're actually back at work, darling.'

'Why?' She asked.

'Because then, however loud the baby's cries are, you won't be able to hear them!'

And He actually had the nerve to laugh.

Honestly, He's as unfeeling as She is.

DAY 25

Change of tactic today. Moved on to a charm offensive.

When She put me down in my cot for my afternoon rest, I smiled up at Her and gurgled like a mountain stream.

It worked. 'Oh, isn't oo an uvvy baby,' She trilled. 'Oo know, Mummy'll miss oo when Mummy's back at work.'

I pressed home my advantage, bringing into play the most powerful weapon in my entire armoury – a new word.

'Mum,' I said. 'Mum. Mum.'

A tear sprang unbidden to Her eye. Oh yes, this is the business, all right.

DAY 26

She is *so* insensitive. After yesterday's heartwarming little incident, She still had the nerve to invite the Juggernaut back to our house 'to begin to get to know Baby'.

We looked at each other with much the same hatred we had shared the first time we met.

'And do you know, Baby's got a clever new trick? Clever new word, haven't oo?' She pointed at Herself. 'Who's this? Who's this?'

Huh. If She thought I was going to behave like a performing animal after the way She'd treated me, She could think again. I turned my head resolutely away.

'Oh, now, come on,' She wheedled. 'Who can oo see over here? Who can oo see over here?'

With great dignity I moved my head round to look at them. Then, very clearly, I pointed at the Juggernaut and said, 'Mum.'

Fifteenth Month

DAY 1

I was plonked down in front of the television at ten o'clock this morning. She's determined I'm going to get hooked on the thing. Honestly – talk about making a rod for her own back.

Anyway, I wasn't going to succumb easily. As soon as She left me for a moment, I rolled over and screamed and squeaked and went through my full attention-grabbing routine.

And do you know what She did? Ignored me completely. Just shut the sitting room door behind Her and went out to make a cup of coffee and phone her friend.

I continued the rolling over, screaming and squeaking, but after about five minutes it was clear She wasn't going to give in, so I stopped. Bored because I had nothing else to do, I started watching the box.

Children's Television? Honestly! What a load of rubbish!

This thing I watched today had a man's hand with a bit of rolled-up cardboard on one finger which I was meant to believe was a mouse. I mean, come *on!*

It was pretty obvious even to me that the only thing the programme had going for it was that it was extremely cheap. Why have real actors or proper animation when you can fob a toddlers' audience off with bits of rolled-up cardboard?

Still, at least it gave me an idea for something to do with a toilet roll. I had to rip all the paper off first, though. I stuffed it down the loo to get rid of it, then I put the cardboard roll on my finger and showed it to Her – I can't imagine why She got so upset.

DAY 2

Watched my parents at breakfast this morning putting bread in the toaster. Looks easy enough. I think I could do that.

After He'd gone to work, I put a slice of bread in *my* toaster.

DAY 3

Bit of a commotion this evening. He'd brought home a video and it wouldn't fit in the slot of the VCR. At least it wouldn't until He took my slice of bread out.

He was furious. I was pretty furious too. It was still just a slice of bread. My toaster doesn't work.

DAY 4

She sat me down in front of Children's Television again after breakfast.

This time it was some pathetic story about dinosaurs going to school dressed in blue and red dungarees. It was told with a few pictures that hardly moved at all, but every now and then something really clever happened like one of the dinosaurs' eyes moved – oh, big deal, I *don't* think.

Do they really want a whole generation of children to grow up believing that dinosaurs

       A) still exist,

       B) go to school, and

       C) wear blue and red dungarees?

DAY 5

She was on about Toilet Training today. I thought of saying, 'I didn't know it was possible to train toilets to do anything', but I don't think She could cope with that level of wit from me at the moment.

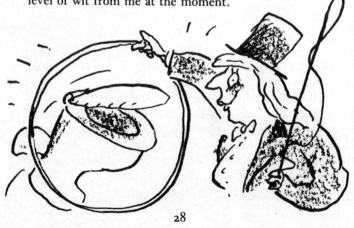

DAY 7

'I've been reading this book . . .' She said after supper this evening.

This is always a bad start. He pretended He hadn't heard and turned up the volume of the television. I pretended I was enormously interested in banging those little brightly coloured plastic rods through the little brightly coloured plastic table with the little brightly coloured plastic hammer. Since I have made a point of ignoring this mindless 'Educational' toy from the moment I was given it, I thought my sudden interest might distract Her.

No such luck. 'It's got some very interesting things to say about Toilet Training,' She continued.

He knew He was beaten straight away – just meekly flicked the television to 'mute' and turned to face Her as if He could think of nothing more fascinating in the world than a discussion of Toilet Training. He's such a hypocrite – He even put on His deeply interested face and said, 'Oh, really, dear?'

'It says,' She went on, 'that though some authorities don't think you should start training till the child's two, many toddlers benefit from earlier encouragement.'

'Oh,' He said.

'It also says that, round fifteen months, the baby will start to make a connection between the bodily sensations and the product.'

He looked blank. Not difficult – it's His natural expression. 'Could you run that past me once again?' He asked. 'Which bodily sensations and what product are we talking about here?'

'The bodily sensations are urinating and straining and the product is, erm . . .' She giggled coyly '. . . Pee or Poo.'

Pee or Poo? What is this? They sound like cartoon characters on Children's Television.

'Sorry . . . I'm still not with you.' Oh, He can be thick sometimes. 'This "making a connection" business . . . ?'

'When the baby starts to make a connection between the bodily sensations and the product . . .'

'The Pee or Poo . . . ?'

'Exactly. Well, when that happens, the whole business of Toilet Training becomes a lot simpler.'

'Oh,' He said.

As one, they turned to look at me. I did nothing. I'm not going to give them the satisfaction of seeing me make the connection. Of course I *know*. I've known from the start that all that grunting and straining leads to a warm soggy glow in the nappy area, but I'm jolly well not going to let them know I know. Am I?

DAY 8

Watched TV again this morning. It was that man with a bit of toilet roll round his finger. Still didn't look like a mouse, but it was quite fun. I wonder what *he* does with the toilet paper?

DAY 11

Things are getting ominous. She got the Juggernaut round this morning. Thought I'd made it obvious the idea's not going to work, but She still seems determined go through with Her attempt to abandon me.

She announced that She'd show the Mother's Help what She called 'the pattern of my day'. So I made damn

30

sure my day didn't have any pattern. I refused to go down for either of my daytime sleeps, I regurgitated all my meals, and got through a whole box of nappies.

I'm still hoping that the Juggernaut will cry off in horror.

DAY 15

The Juggernaut just doesn't care.

It's different with my mum. Because She's seen me from Day One, and because I'm Hers, I can trigger off all Her anxieties and get Her going any time I want to.

So when She sees me going into my I-am-either-choking-or-beginning-to-get-a-high-temperature routine, even though She's seen it a hundred times before, a little potential panic starts up in Her and eventually She comes rushing along to check me out.

But with the Juggernaut . . . when I go into the routine, she either ignores me completely or looks at me as if to say, 'Well, let's just wait a bit and see if you really do choke or get a high temperature.'

DAY 16

The Juggernaut came again today, and She actually had the nerve to go out shopping 'for some clothes for next week. I still don't fit into most of the stuff I used to wear before I had the baby.'

This reminder that, if nothing else, I've at least managed to ruin Her figure, did not bring me its customary warm glow. My thoughts were shadowed by a hideous anxiety. What's this 'next week' business? Can it be true that She's actually planning to go back to work as soon as that?

Before She left, She showed the Juggernaut all my favourite toys and games. 'Baby'll play with these for hours,' She chirped merrily.

And did I touch one of them all the time She was out? What do you think?

DAY 17

My mum got the Juggernaut to take me to the supermarket today. I started off by behaving perfectly: didn't reach out for anything, didn't grab anything off the shelves, didn't eat anything out of the trolley. Was a right little goody-goody, in fact . . . until we got to the checkout.

Then I grabbed handfuls of all the things they have stacked up there for impulse buying – bars of chocolate, family magazines, boxes of matches, batteries. Tore, slobbered over or generally defaced as much as I could in the time available.

Added £17.49 to the bill. Not bad . . .

DAY 18

'Not worried about leaving the baby, are you?' I heard Him asking Her this evening. 'You know, when you go back to work . . . ?'

'Good Lord, no,' She said in an airy voice that carried a gratifying undercurrent of anxiety.

'Won't be any problems,' He reassured.

'Course not,' She agreed briskly. 'Bringing up children is a continual process of growing away from each other. Separation can actually improve the parent/child relationship.'

Clearly She's been reading one of those childcare books again.

'And you won't miss the baby?' He asked with tender concern.

'Good heavens, no!' She replied – rather too readily for my taste. 'Because, you see, the important thing is that the baby and I will spend Quality Time together.'

What the hell . . . ? What on earth is Quality Time? Tell you one thing – whatever it is, I'll be the one who decides on the quality, and I'll be the one who picks the time.

DAY 19

She is just *so* devious. During the past weeks She's taken to peeling and quartering an apple for me at bedtime. Now I'm quite partial to a piece of nice crunchy apple.

33

I like the way it breaks up when you suck it, and I enjoy smearing bits over my sleeping suit and duvet. But it wasn't till today that I realized I had been the victim of an evil plot.

She's only been giving me the apple to take my mind off my customary night-time breastfeed. She reckoned that if I had an apple to play with, and if I wasn't stopped from mashing it into my bedclothes, I'd forget about my little snack from Her.

And the infuriating thing is – She was right. It's all part of Her callous masterplan to put as much space between us as possible.

I have been weaned by deceit.

DAY 22

I am an orphan.

That's how it feels. This morning it happened. She has gone back to work, leaving me, desolate and alone, with only the Juggernaut for company.

I spent the morning pottering wistfully about the house, peering into cupboards and behind pieces of furniture, looking for my lost mother. It was a pitiful sight.

I spent the afternoon sobbing quietly. All right, I may have said the odd hurtful thing about Her in the past, but, you know, today I really did miss having Her around – and not just to torment either.

Did I get any sympathy from the Juggernaut, I hear you cry. Huh. I assume that was a rhetorical question.

And when my mum came home, looking drained and shattered, the wretched creature actually had the nerve to lie to Her.

'How's Baby been?' She asked the moment She was through the door.

'Oh, fine,' came the reply.

'Hasn't missed me at all?' She asked anxiously.

'Good heavens, *no*!'

Ooh, they're such liars, grown-ups.

'Now oo will be a good baby, won't oo?' She said after the Juggernaut had gone. 'Mummy's very tired – very, very tired. I'd forgotten how exhausting work was – and I really do need a good night's sleep. Oo'll let me have that, won't oo then?'

I'm sorry. But after the day I'd had, I couldn't, could I?

I screamed and bawled the whole night through. She didn't get more than ten minutes' consecutive sleep at any point.

Eventually, in desperation at four-thirty, She opened Her nightdress and clamped me to Her breast.

Not much of a milk-flow yet, but I'm sure I can get it going again with a bit of dedicated sucking.

DAY 24

The Juggernaut had the nerve to take me out shopping at ten o'clock this morning. I screamed and gave her absolute hell. Actually managed to throw a whole box of eggs out of the supermarket trolley. All but two smashed.

'I don't know why you're behaving like this,' she kept saying.

I'm afraid she isn't terribly bright. It was perfectly obvious why.

I WAS MISSING CHILDREN'S TELE-
VISION.

I actually wanted to know what was happening to the
mouse made out of toilet roll.

Awful to admit it, but I *care*.

DAY 26

Got to the end of Her first week at work. The Juggernaut
handed me over the moment She was through the door
and vanished with a shouted, 'See you Monday.'

She looked at me. 'God, I'm dead,' She said. 'I'm just
going to collapse for the evening. Now you'll be a good
baby and have a nice early night, won't you . . . ?'

Just a minute. She's finished work for the week.
Where's all that Quality Time She promised me?

DAY 27

Saturday. Today was clearly going to be the day for
Quality Time. She looked more human when She woke
up, and Her first words were, 'Now isn't oo an uvvy,
lucky little baby? Mummy's going to devote every minute
of today to looking after oo.'

She *needed* every minute, I saw to that. By the end
of the day She was a gibbering wreck, wondering with
appalled terror what kind of monster She'd spawned.

A thought struck Her as She was once again trying to
get me off to sleep, and She said to Him, 'You don't think

the Mother's Help is actually encouraging bad habits in Baby, do you?'

'Natural for Baby to play up a bit after your first week back at work,' He said reassuringly.

'Maybe, but I've never known behaviour as bad as this,' She said, confirming my own assessment of my prowess.

This is good, I thought, this is very promising. If I can foster the doubt that they're leaving their precious child in the hands of someone morally unsuitable, then I may soon be able to get this ridiculous going-back-to-work decision reversed.

Huh. I'll give Her Quality Time.

Sixteenth Month

DAY 1

Part of this Quality Time nonsense She keeps on about now involves Her reading me a bedtime story. I'm quite keen on this because:

A) It ensures I have Her absolute undivided attention,

B) Books do tear very agreeably when you suddenly grab hold of them.

DAY 2

I've been given lots of books but so far, except for ripping up one or two, I've ignored them completely.

But now She's reading me a Quality Time bedtime story every night, I've decided to take more interest. In fact, I've decided to have a favourite book.

Wasn't hard to choose which. I picked the one His mother gave me last Christmas, and I could tell from Her expression when I unwrapped the thing that She hated it.

I insisted on that one tonight. Actually, it was so boring I fell asleep while She was reading it. Rats! I hate it when that happens.

DAY 4

I said another new word today. When the Juggernaut arrived for the morning handover, She pointed at her and asked, 'Well, now, who's this come to see oo then?'

Triumphantly I bellowed out my new word. 'Bum!'

'Oh, isn't that clever!' my mother cooed. 'Baby's trying to say "Beth!"'

No, Baby isn't. Baby knows exactly what Baby's trying to say.

DAY 5

Insisted again on my favourite bedtime story, the one His mother gave me. It's about some perky little creep in a red jacket and a funny hat who goes around helping people all the time. Pretty yucky, I agree, but it does have that vital quality which is guaranteed to drive parents mad – too many words for the number of pictures, and I make sure she reads every one of them . . . time and time again.

DAY 6

My anti-Juggernaut tactics for today involved the use of yet another new word. It's one I've been thinking about for quite a while – 'want'.

I whinged, screamed and hit out at her all day. 'Want Mum!' I kept bawling inconsolably. 'Want Mum! Want Mum!'

This was actually an important development in my linguistic skills. For the first time I was stringing two words together and creating a phrase. Quite advanced.

Many babies do not manage to combine words until they're eighteen months or even older.

But, of course, the Juggernaut didn't notice my precocity. I made her life such a misery that she didn't have time to.

By the time She came back from work, the Juggernaut was nearly on her knees. I've never known a human body move so quickly as when I was thrust into Her arms.

'You take it!' the Juggernaut said fiercely. 'Been a right little bugger all day. God, you know . . . this job makes walking backwards up Everest look easy.'

My mum was instantly worried. 'You don't mean you're not going to stay, do you?'

I had a brief moment of hope, but . . . no such luck. Fixing me with a baleful eye, the Juggernaut replied, 'By no means. Let me tell you, I regard looking after your baby as a *challenge*.'

Oh dear.

I whinged, screamed and hit out at Her all evening – and for much of the night. 'Want Bum!' I kept bawling inconsolably. 'Want Bum! Want Bum!'

DAY 8

Another land–speed record was broken this morning as She thrust me into the Juggernaut's arms almost before the girl was through the front door. 'Here she is! Here's Beth!' my mother hissed at me through gritted teeth. '*Now* are you satisfied?'

I wriggled and twisted and tried to get away. 'Want Mum!' I began bawling inconsolably. 'Want Mum! Want Mum!'

DAY 9

Today I gave in and took my First Step.

And I made a point of doing it mid-morning so that only the Juggernaut witnessed it.

When She got home and was told of the advance, I am glad to say She got a bit snuffly and emotional.

I'll show Her what She's missing by this ill-considered rush back to work.

DAY 11

Sunday. This morning He started digging a hole in the garden. For a moment I thought it meant the cat had died, but no such luck.

She took me to the kitchen window to watch Him working and said, 'It's for oo.'

I burst into tears. Well, wouldn't anyone in the circumstances? I know we've had our differences over the last few months, but burying me alive does seem a rather extreme form of revenge.

She cuddled me. 'Don't cry, silly Baby. Daddy's making oo a sandpit. A sandpit for oo to play lots of uvvy games in.'

I perked up immediately. Be great to have a sandpit. One of the first 'uvvy games' I planned to play in it was burying the cat alive.

When He came in for lunch, He was all covered in mud, but very pleased with Himself. 'I feel really close to the soil,' He announced. 'Nothing like a tough morning's manual work. I feel fitter than I have for years. All that digging's given me a thirst, though. I could murder a beer.'

He murdered a good few beers over lunch and kept telling me how great it would be when I'd got my sandpit. 'You can make pies and castles and roads and tunnels. Be terrific. And,' He said, turning to Her, 'it's educational too. Really good for them, building things, making things. Develops their practical side, you know.'

'Yes, yes, that's great,' She agreed.

After lunch, He didn't seem that keen on going back to His digging. All those beers He'd murdered, I shouldn't wonder.

And then, when She at last persuaded Him that He really ought to get on with it, He tried to stand up and collapsed in agony. 'Ooh, my back's gone,' He moaned. 'All that digging.'

While She helped Him slowly up the stairs to lie down, I decided I'd crawl into the garden and inspect His excavations.

It was dead good, the hole. Beautifully muddy. And it had worms in it. Good and soft, worms. All nice and gooey when you chew them.

After I'd had a few worms, I started in on the mud. It was lovely – and not just to eat. You can squidge it round into lumps and dig holes in it and smear it all over the place – smashing.

I'd been cheerfully amusing myself for twenty minutes or so, when suddenly I heard a wail. 'Oh, no!' She screamed as She hurtled over to scoop me up. 'What on earth do you think you're doing?'

I didn't bother to answer. Well, it was obvious, wasn't it? I was making pies and castles and roads and tunnels, just like He wanted me to. I was doing something educational. I was developing my practical side.

But did She see it like that? Oh no. 'Don't you ever dare do that again!' She shouted. 'It's disgusting and filthy and incredibly bad for you!'

Why are grown-ups so inconsistent?

DAY 12

He was off work today with his bad back. She said She really wished He hadn't started on the sandpit. The garden looked such a mess. She'd have to get the oddjob man in as usual to finish yet another job He'd botched up. He said over His dead body.

DAY 15

Making an incredible amount of fuss – He always does when He claims to be ill – He went back to work today, telling Her He'd finish the sandpit at the weekend and, whatever She did, She was not to call in the oddjob man. She promised She wouldn't.

The minute He had hobbled painfully out of the front door, She was on the phone to the oddjob man.

He arrived within half an hour and was let in by the Juggernaut. By the end of the day I was the proud possessor of a sandpit.

DAY 17

Saturday. She kitted me out in boots and waterproof gear and placed me in the sandpit. It was good fun. All morning I patted little mounds of sand into pies. And every time I did it, She said, 'Isn't oo a clever baby then! Ooh, what a lovely pie oo's made then!'

At lunchtime I was stripped off and hosed down. Then She sat me in my high chair and placed a dish of mashed potatoes and gravy in front of me.

I started making mounds out of this and patting them into pies.

But did I get any congratulations this time? I assume you're joking.

No 'Isn't oo a clever baby then! Ooh, what a lovely pie oo's made then!' – oh no. Instead, She went all purple and started going on about what a naughty baby I was. Not fair.

DAY 18

Sunday. 'We're going to do something very exciting after lunch,' She said today.

Oh yes? I wondered what it'd be this time. Concorde landing in the garden? Princess Di making a rare personal appearance? My expectations were not high. She has a habit of describing the most incredibly boring things as exciting.

So I was pretty wary as the end of my lunch approached. I spun the last bit out. Pushed the food around my plate, then pushed the plate around my tray.

Suddenly, unperturbed by my delaying tactics, She whisked me out of the chair, swabbed me down and held me in this totally immobilizing one-armed grip which I swear she must have learnt from a martial arts manual.

Then in one easy movement She whipped off my dungarees and nappy. What is going on here? I thought. It's extremely undignified for someone of my age to be carted around naked from the waist down.

Just before this sudden offensive, I'd been on the verge of doing what I frequently do straight after lunch . . . but I certainly wasn't going to do it now. Doing a Poo without having a nice, clean nappy to deposit it in takes away all the fun. It makes you feel a bit like a seagull flying over a totally deserted beach.

So I clenched everything and tried to think of something else. Something mechanical, something mathematical. Oh yes . . . How many different ways did I know of antagonizing the cat? That'd take my mind off it.

Right, there was pulling its tail . . . poking a finger in its eye . . . grabbing a handful of fur on its tummy . . . sticking my thumb up its—

My concentration was broken when, reaching down casually behind the table, She produced an object to strike terror into the heart of any right-thinking baby.

It was a potty.

The potty Her mother had given Her just before my first birthday.

Then I understood what She was up to. But She wasn't going to catch me so easily. The minute I saw the potty I toddled across the room (I'm getting quite good at this

46

walking business now) and went straight into the first grunt of a major Poo, targeting the kitchen floor which She'd only just cleaned.

But She can be devious, too. As soon as She heard me grunt, She lowered me with great rapidity down on to the potty, so that I was straddling it with my bottom squashed hard against the cold plastic.

Instantly my brain flashed clenching instructions to my buttocks, and I tried furiously to think about anything other than doing a Poo. I wasn't going to give Her the satisfaction of a direct hit in the potty first time.

Rubbing jam into the cat's back . . . wrapping sellotape round its tail . . . throwing wooden bricks at it . . . smearing yoghurt round the edge of the cat-flap . . .

'Come on, I know you want to,' She cooed in a seductive voice. 'You want to do a nice big Poo in the potty, don't you . . . ?'

'NO!' I screamed. 'NO!'

If I'd hoped the use of a relatively new word would once again strike Her dumb with admiration, I was quickly disillusioned.

'*Yes*,' She said. 'You mean *yes*.'

I was struck dumb by this appalling infringement of civil liberties. Can't adults understand – when a baby says 'No', a baby *means* 'No'.

47

'Come on,' She continued soothingly. 'You want to do a big Poo in the potty, don't you?'

The brainwashing technique only made me more determined. I executed a sudden lateral movement, jerking free from Her grasp, and managed to tip sideways so that I lay on the floor.

Unfortunately, the potty, drawn to me by suction, remained stuck to my bottom.

I screamed. How can a baby be expected to retain any self-respect when its parents keep forcing it into such undignified postures?

But this particular indignity was quickly ended. The buttock-seal mercifully gave and, with a slight 'pflumph' noise, the potty dropped off me.

It was the perfect moment for the Poo.

But you can't just do it to order. It takes a while to build up concentration, and I was hardly into the first preliminary grunt before She again whisked me up, righted the potty and started to lower me on to it.

I clenched, counted more cat-terrorizing techniques, and resorted to a new tactic – kicking out wildly with my legs as if pedalling an invisible bicycle.

This was very effective, making it completely impossible for Her to sit me on the potty. And before long one of my flailing legs did as I'd hoped, and sent the thing spinning across the room.

(NB: I must bear this in mind for the future. Just think how effective sending a *full* potty spinning across the room will be.)

There was no doubt I was gaining the upper hand. With no potty in position for Her to lower me on to, She'd have to give up. Also, She was beginning to feel the strain physically. There is nothing that will do a mother's back in so effectively as bending down holding a furiously pedalling baby a few inches above the ground.

She gave up and sat me on the floor, moving away to stretch her aching spine.

My timing was perfect. A quick grunt and there was a healthy dollop all over the clean floor. Before She had time to get me away, I bottom-shuffled a bit to spread it around.

There was no room for argument. I had triumphantly won the day.

DAY 20

No further attempts to get me near the potty, I'm glad to say. The chief reason for this was that She was off work, confined to bed with a bad back.

Seventeenth Month

DAY 4

This evening He found me trying to poke a fork into an electrical socket. 'No!' he said. 'No! Naughty Baby! Not a sensible thing to do!'

He was dead right, of course. It wasn't sensible. For the simple reason that the average fork doesn't fit into an electrical socket.

Never mind, I'll just have to find something that does.

DAY 5

Tried poking a metal ballpoint pen (Her favourite Parker, actually) into an electrical socket. That didn't fit either. Don't worry, I'll keep trying.

DAY 6

Toddling around in the kitchen this morning, I got interested in the cat-flap. It's just the right height for me, and makes a very satisfactory clattering noise when you push it open and let go.

But then I ran into problems. After bashing it open and closed for a while, I decided to see if my head would

fit through. The good news is: it did. The bad news is: the flap then slipped down and immobilized me. Now I know what it feels like to face the guillotine.

My head was in the garden, the rest of me in the kitchen. What made it worse was that the cat, about to enter, saw me and clearly recognized a sitting target. I screamed and bellowed as it approached, sharpening its claws, and the Juggernaut only just arrived in time to save me. I never thought I'd be so pleased to see her.

DAY 7

Tried poking a wooden cocktail stick into an electrical socket.

The good news is: it fitted.

The bad news is: nothing happened.

I'll try again.

DAY 8

My fascination with the cat-flap won't go away. I was playing with it this morning when another unpleasantness occurred. As I nuzzled up to the flap, testing how far I could push my head through before it got trapped, the cat, in flight from next door's black tom, launched itself from outside in one of its kamikaze leaps.

The edge of the flap caught me on the chin, I sprawled backwards, the cat landed plonk on my chest.

And the beastly animal had the nerve to grin. I will be revenged.

DAY 9

I didn't have to wait long to get back at the cat. Simple, really. All I did was check the creature was not in the house, push a Giant Size box of washing powder flush up against the cat-flap, and wait.

Wonderfully satisfying, you know – the sound of a tom-pursued cat slamming itself at thirty miles an hour face first into a closed cat-flap.

DAY 10

This evening He brought a video home. *The Hand that Rocks the Cradle*. I thought it looked interesting, so, about an hour after they'd put me to bed, I summoned them up to my bedroom on the pretext of teething agony.

They were too knackered to stay with me till I went back to sleep, so they brought me down to the sitting room.

They were also, I'm glad to say, too knackered to take me back upstairs once I'd stopped crying. Which meant I watched most of *The Hand that Rocks the Cradle*. Very interesting.

DAY 11

I had a nasty accident this morning. Hurtling across the room in an attempt to grab hold of the cat (I wanted to find out what'd happen if I poked its tail into an electrical socket), I ran straight into the corner of the dining room table. (Why they make tables exactly the height of the average toddler's temple I will never understand.) A lump like an egg immediately appeared above my right eyebrow.

Needless to say, I bawled my head off. This was rewarded by the usual perfunctory cuddle from the Juggernaut, accompanied by the words, 'Who's a silly baby then?' – which I found less than helpful.

Huh. If my mother'd been here when I crashed into the table, I'd have been whipped into Casualty before you could say X-Ray, and spent an achingly sentimental night in the Children's Ward with both parents in anguished vigil beside me.

By the time She got back from work, I looked like I'd gone fifteen rounds with Mike Tyson, but She didn't seem that bothered. Perhaps the fact that I'd been pottering around quite cheerfully for at least five hours since the accident diluted her instinctive anxiety.

'What happened?' She asked.

'Oh,' the Juggernaut replied casually. 'Chased the cat and walked into the side of the dining room table.'

'I see,' said She, apparently satisfied.

But I caught a look in Her eye which could turn out to be quite promising. It was a momentary doubt, almost a suspicion, which I think I can play on in the future.

Good video, that *Hand that Rocks the Cradle*.

DAY 14

This morning I deliberately walked into the edge of His desk and got a nice graze on my left temple.

All day I planned the reproachful look I was going to give the Juggernaut when She asked her what'd happened. I would play on my mother's natural neurosis, make Her really wonder what kind of monster She was leaving her precious offspring with. I reckoned the Juggernaut'd be out on her ear within the week.

Then my mother would have to give up this work nonsense and do what She should be doing – devoting her every waking minute to pandering to my slightest whim.

It all started off according to plan. When She got home, She whisked me up in Her arms and instantly saw the new injury. 'Goodness, you've been in the wars,' She said. Then, turning to the Juggernaut, asked, 'What happened?'

'Only walked into your old man's desk,' the girl replied casually.

I should have got an Oscar for my look – no, really. It was absolutely brilliant – full of reproach, doubt, pain and, yes, sheer, naked fear.

But do you know what . . . ? She wasn't even looking at me when I did it. She just put me down on the floor and said airily, 'Oh, oo'll soon learn not to do that again.' Then She had the nerve to add, 'Won't oo, oo silly baby?'

And She went into the kitchen announcing that She was gasping for a drink.

What's going on here? Am I losing my touch?

DAY 16

Sunday. Today I found the perfect thing to stick into an electrical socket. They'd had kebabs for supper last night and the metal skewers were left on the draining board. While they were both out in the garden (trying to catch the cat to put a flea collar on it), I toddled into the kitchen, managed to manoeuvre a chair up to the sink, climb up on it and take one of the skewers.

Then a quick scurry to the sitting room to find my favourite electrical socket.

Disaster. Do you know what He'd gone and done? He'd only fixed a plastic cover over the socket. Not just over that one either; as I discovered through the day, He'd put them on every electrical socket in the house.

Huh. It often seems to me that the only reason parents are put on this earth is to ensure that children don't have any fun at all!

DAY 22

There is sort of a tidemark round this house, and it keeps moving upwards. Before my parents had me (an impossible concept, I agree – what did the world revolve around then, I ask myself?) they used to store things on the floor. There were plant-pots, books, the CD player and all kinds of stuff – I remember seeing it when I was tiny.

Then, as I began to crawl – and after a few smashed plant-pots, shredded books and Ribena-drenched CD equipment – all their possessions started to move up the walls till they were out of reach of a baby who still had to keep one hand on the floor when reaching upwards.

But, as soon as I was able to pull myself up on things, the possibilities for mayhem once again increased. Vases were toppled from tables, ornaments from shelves, glasses from cupboards. And I discovered that invaluable law of physics – you know the one – that if you hang on to a tablecloth with all your weight, eventually everything on top of it will come smashing down to the floor.

So once again the tidemark of my parents' breakable possessions moved further up the wall.

Now I can walk – well, all right, wobble and clamber – my horizon for devastation has been raised once again. Luckily, they are, as yet, blissfully unaware of this.

I won't rush things. My next orgy of destruction can wait. But I have something *rather* special in mind.

DAY 24

She's got this collection of china cats in the sitting room that I've had my eye on for ages. Apparently She was given the first one when She was about five and ever since, for birthdays, Christmases, etc., people who hadn't the imagination to think of anything else have stumped up yet another china cat. Must be over twenty of them now.

The cats have not moved up the walls with everything else. No, they've always been very precious and have had pride of place on a special shelf quite a way out of my reach, but now I can walk . . .

DAY 26

This morning, while the Juggernaut was swearing at the tumble drier (I wonder if that pair of pliers I popped in has anything to do with why it's jammed), I measured myself up against the shelf which houses Her china cat collection.

Yes. On tiptoe I can reach quite easily.

But no rush. I am determined to choose the moment of maximum impact. And that means when She's here. And He's here too. I'm not going to waste something like this on the Juggernaut.

DAY 30

Sunday. The moment has arrived. And, to make things even better, it's Her birthday.

This means they've embarked on one of their riskier enterprises – inviting both sets of grandparents to the house at the same time. Experience has shown that this is invariably a social event to make Genghis Khan's dinner parties look quite civilized, but do they learn . . . ?

They normally reckon they can take some of the curse off these ghastly occasions if they've got some new trick of mine to demonstrate. Today She offered the spectacle of me sitting in a high chair without a tray in front, so that I actually had my bowl of food on the same table as the rest of them.

The experiment wasn't a total success, because I kept alternately slipping down on to the floor and slumping forward into my food.

The advantage from my point of view, however, was that the new chair enabled me to get out at will – something which had never been possible from the old high chair (whose design had clearly been based on that popular medieval instrument of torture, the stocks).

Inevitably, as the meal chuntered on, and as they all drank more, they took less and less notice of me. By the time they had blearily reached the coffee stage, no one saw me slip down from my chair and totter off into the sitting room.

All my preparations paid off. I was quick and totally devastating.

I pulled myself up with one hand and with the other cut a swathe through the array of china cats. As they hit the ground, they made a delicious smashing noise.

Inevitably this brought the grown-ups rushing in from the dining room.

My mother was instantly in tears, wailing that I'd destroyed Her most precious possessions.

His mother then said they were only a bunch of plaster cats, not that much to make such a fuss about. Her mother waded in, saying that they were *china* cats, not plaster, and the fact that His mother couldn't tell the difference was just another reflection of the complete lack of taste shown by every member of His family.

This lit the fuse for all the old family arguments to explode once again. The afternoon ended with both sets of grandparents stomping off in high dudgeon, and a furious row between my parents which continued for the rest of the day – and probably most of the night.

It has to be said that when I want to make an impact, *I make an impact*.

Eighteenth Month

DAY 7

She started talking to Him again this evening about Parent and Toddler Groups. Diversionary tactics were clearly called for, so I went into a great grunt-and-groan routine and managed to fill my nappy very satisfactorily.

'Doing a Poo,' She said excitedly as soon as I started. Then, looking very seriously into my face, She intoned, 'You are doing a Poo. You are doing a Poo.'

For a moment I thought perhaps She was trying to hypnotize me, but then I realized this was part of the great campaign to help me make the connection between 'the bodily sensations and the product'.

To make the point even more firmly, She said, '*You* are doing a Poo.'

She kept on with this while She carried me up to the bathroom and changed my nappy. 'You've done a Poo, haven't you? Clever Baby. *You*'ve done a Poo. *You*'ve done a Poo.'

When I was all clean and dressed again, She picked me up and looked at me fondly. 'Now do you understand?' She asked. '*Who*'s done a Poo?'

I smiled at Her knowingly and pointed at the cat.

DAY 9

I was taken out by the Juggernaut today to visit another baby. This one was smaller than me – very tiny actually – and could hardly even crawl. Its mother got some finger paints out for me to play with. Then she and the Juggernaut went off to have a cup of coffee in the kitchen.

Have you ever seen a tiny baby entirely covered in finger paint?

DAY 11

'Just going to put Baby down,' She said to Him, as She scooped me up off the sofa this evening.

I really don't like this expression 'put down' which they always use when it's time to go to bed. The only other context in which I've heard them use the phrase was when they were discussing what they'd do with the cat if its incontinence got worse. They would take it to the vet and 'have it put down'.

I think my paranoia about the expression is justified – particularly if incontinence is one of the reasons for having it done to you.

Anyway, tonight when I was put down, I suddenly realized that I was also being 'put away'. My cot is a prison. My parents put me in it every night, with any amount of cooing, then pull the side up and reckon I'm safely incarcerated till the morning.

I can shout and scream and rattle the bars and they may eventually come to settle me, but as far as they're concerned, once I'm in there I'm banged up for the night. And till now I've gone along with this. I have accepted it as a fair cop and done my porridge. I have never tasted the night-time freedom that exists outside the bars of my cot.

Hm. I'm too sleepy to do anything about it tonight, but a new escape plan is forming in my tiny brain.

DAY 12

I am not without experience of escape. Those of you fortunate enough to have read *How to be a Little Sod* will recall the epic breakout from my playpen in my Eleventh Month. On that occasion I managed to get through the bars. My cot's construction is too solid to make that a possibility, and its base is considerably higher above the ground than my playpen's was, so the current escape poses new problems.

On the other hand, since I can get about much more easily now, I'm sure I can break out somehow. This evening I did a recce.

Pulling myself upright on the bars is no problem. But when I get there I find the top rail is at about my chest height. Clearly what I have to do from that position is to raise myself with my arms as if doing pull-ups in a gym. Then, by leaning forward, I will reach a point where my centre of gravity is over the rail, enabling me neatly to somersault to freedom.

That at least is the theory. The practice, on this evening's showing, is going to prove more difficult.

The trouble is that my arms just aren't strong enough. All this walking has developed my leg muscles, but I haven't much strength in my upper body.

Never mind. Rome wasn't built in a day. I will persevere.

DAY 13

I spent the day working on my upper body. I pulled myself up on anything I could get hold of, and dangled there for as long as my arms would let me.

When I was put into my cot in the evening, I tried more pull-ups, but my arms were too sore and I ended up crying.

She came in to comfort me, though not with the spontaneous warmth and sympathy I had hoped for.

'I know you're just trying it on,' She said. 'You're quite capable of going off to sleep without all this fuss. Soon, you know, I'm just going to leave you when you play up in the evenings. I'm not here to be at your beck and call all the time.'

That from a woman who has callously abandoned her offspring for the last three months, without a backward glance, on the fatuous pretext of going back to work. God, she's heartless.

DAY 15

I am nothing if not tenacious. In spite of the pain, I persisted all day with my upper body training, and was rewarded by a small but definite lift-off when I tried a pull-up on the top rail of my cot this evening.

The triumph was only marred by the fact that I lost my hand-hold and fell heavily against the back bars. The pain caused a quite justifiable outbreak of crying, but all the sympathy I got from Her was more accusations of playing up and threats that She really would leave me 'to stew in my own juice'.

I concentrated on filling my nappy with some really noxious juice to stew in overnight.

DAY 23

I have been a fool. All this time I've been trying to pull myself over the outer side of my cot (the one that slides up and down), and I hadn't noticed until this evening that there is another possible escape route.

On the rigid side of my cot, about halfway up its railings, is fixed what is laughingly called an 'Activity Centre'.

This is a plastic board on to which various brightly coloured dials, bells, pingers, switches, etc. are attached.

The idea is that a baby will sit cooing away in its cot, deriving hours of harmless fun from dialling the dials, ringing the bells, pinging the pingers, clicking the switches, etc.

Well . . . I mean, I tried it when I first got the thing. I dialled a dial. I rang a bell. I pinged a pinger. I clicked a switch. I etcetera'd an etc.

But, quite honestly, when you've done it once, you've done it. I quickly wrote the whole thing off as useless.

Until today. Today I suddenly saw its purpose. It could double as a step. If I grasped the top of my cot and moved my foot up to rest on the Activity Centre, it would only require a small effort to heave my body upwards and project myself over the top – and freedom!

My first try this evening wasn't entirely successful. Just when I got to the point where one leg was on the Activity Centre and the other waving in the void, I lost my balance and went crashing down on my face.

This, naturally, provoked crying. And an angry appearance from my mother. Unfortunately, my painful crash-landing hadn't left any visible marks, so once again I got all the accusations about 'playing up' and 'trying it on'.

She tucked me under my duvet with what I thought was excessive force. 'And the next time you cry in the evening,' was Her parting shot, 'I'm just going to leave you to cry. So remember, if you cry tomorrow evening, nobody's going to come to you till the morning!'

I let all this wash over me. I felt pretty good. Because, although this evening's escape attempt hadn't been successful, I had at least proved that the principle worked.

And tomorrow would be another day.

DAY 24

Didn't bother with the weight training today. My new method of escape doesn't require as much brute strength as the old one. Now it's more a question of balance and timing.

I behaved pretty well with the Juggernaut, and didn't even give my mum too much grief when She came back from work. He was away on business, as she pointed out when She settled me for the night.

'Now Daddy won't be here, so crying's not going to do you any good. He's a big softie and you can get round him, but you can't get round *me*. If you cry tonight, I'll know you're just playing up, and I will leave you till the morning. It's the only way we're going to end this vicious circle of antisocial behaviour.'

Huh. She'd been reading one of her childcare books again. I can always tell.

It was probably from the book that She got her other innovation of the evening – a nightlight. It was a little squat candle thing, housed in a hideous ceramic mushroom house. Having lit this device with great ceremony,

She placed it on a table some way away from the cot.

Then, with an expression of evil glee, She gave me a kiss, said, 'Night, night. See you in the morning,' went out . . . AND CLOSED THE DOOR.

It had all been planned. I felt betrayed and screamed out my fury at her base deception.

Sadly, there was no reaction to my bawling, so after a while I shut up. No doubt, downstairs She was congratulating Herself on a job well done.

The nightlight gave as much illumination as the crack in the door to the landing, so I could see quite enough to put my plan into action.

I pulled myself to my feet, put my hands on the rim of the cot and did a few preparatory bounces on the mattress. Then I stretched my left leg until it found firm purchase on the top of the Activity Centre.

Keeping cool and not rushing the manoeuvre, I lifted myself upwards. My free leg waved dangerously in the air for a moment, but then, following a plan I had worked out during the day, I moved it round till it joined the other one.

Then, all I had to do was push myself forward. The front of my sleeping suit slid across the top of the cot wall. Soon my navel pressed against the rail and I was balanced, almost rocking on the edge of the cot.

I gave a great heave with both legs, and at the same time loosened the grip of my hands. I was airborne. At that moment I knew what it was to 'taste freedom'.

The next moment I knew what it was to taste landing face-first on the floor from a vast height. It really hurt. This time my screams were absolutely genuine.

But they got no response. I bellowed, I howled, I did the full Temper Tantrum routine. Nothing. She was sticking to Her guns.

The pain subsided. I crawled across the floor until I found a pile of towels. I curled up on them. Pressing my face into their softness, I could feel a very satisfying lump emerging on my forehead. I dozed.

A little later, I was alerted by the sound of Her footsteps coming up the stairs. They paused outside my door.

Suddenly I decided it would suit my purposes better if She didn't come in. I raised the volume and evenness and peacefulness of my breathing, and was rewarded by the sound of Her saying, 'Oh, there's a good baby. See, I told you you wouldn't be able to get round me.'

I went back to sleep.

DAY 25

I slept very well and woke up before Her. I lay for a moment, reminding myself of where I was and how I'd got there. My injury didn't hurt at all, though I could feel that the lump had grown into a great egg on my forehead.

Then I had a brainwave for the final refinement of my plan. I moved across the room and knocked the hideous ceramic mushroom off the table. It shattered satisfyingly, and its guttering nightlight was extinguished in the fall.

I didn't go back to my comfy nest of towels, but instead arranged myself awkwardly in the middle of the floor.

Through the wall, I heard the sound of Her clock radio switching itself on, and immediately started crying. Not the full-voiced bellowing of a baby who has just woken up, but the exhausted, attenuated grizzle of a baby who has been crying all night.

She came through quickly, saying, 'There – you've been a good baby. I told you we didn't need all that playing up and . . .'

Her words trickled away as She saw me. I looked up at Her with one pathetic eye.

Instantly She was on the floor by my side. 'Oh, my God!' She cried. 'How long have you been there? And look at that bruise on your forehead! Oh no! I didn't know you could get out of the cot. Oh, and the nightlight . . . You could have been burnt to death!'

Though I say it myself, I thought the whole exercise was brilliant.

So upset and guilty was She that She rang the Juggernaut to put her off and stayed home to look after me Herself. Throughout the day I managed to plumb ever deeper depths of appalling behaviour, and She took it all like a lamb.

I even made such a fuss in the evening that She took me into their bed (He was still away on business), and, once there, She let me have a breastfeed. There wasn't any milk left, so it ended up as a bit of a nibble – or, to be strictly accurate, a chew. A few more nights like this, you know, and I think I could get the milk flowing again.

Serve her right to think She can outwit me.

And the great continuing advantage of the campaign is – I now know I can get out of my cot. And they know I can too. Nervous days ahead for my parents, I'd say.

Nineteenth Month

DAY 5

The Juggernaut has organized a Parent and Toddler Group. Three children came round to the house with their Mother's Helps this morning.

I took a dim view of this. I don't want other children playing with my toys. Also, they all very quickly caught on to the idea of hitting me back.

And, anyway, it wasn't a Parent and Toddler Group. It was a Mother's Help and Toddler Group, gathering together a bunch of pathetic children whose parents have abandoned them while they swan off and enjoy themselves at work. And, if they expect me to mix, they'll have to do better than this lot. They were noisy and smelly and – well – some of them hit a lot harder than me.

DAY 12

I've reached an awkward stage of my life. Or, to be more accurate, I should say I've reached an even more awkward stage of my life. Thing is, until now I've really been on three sleeps a day – the big one overnight, and a couple of top-ups mid-morning and afternoon.

I've tried to resist this pattern, because obviously my being asleep gives either Her or the Juggernaut the opportunity to get on with something uninterrupted. But I'm afraid sheer exhaustion always overcomes me eventually and I nod off.

Now, however, things are changing. I don't seem to need as much sleep as I used to.

Today I gave the Juggernaut the first hint of the unpleasantness to come. I'd had my morning nap as usual, but when she put me down after lunch I just didn't feel sleepy. She left with her customary, 'Now you have a nice little rest and let me get on with my work, all right?', and I immediately started to scream.

She didn't respond, because I quite often do this and then, in spite of my best intentions, just drift off to sleep after a few minutes. But I kept up the racket and at last she had to come upstairs. She tried settling me three or four times before giving up and taking me back downstairs with her.

Then I discovered something I'd suspected for some time. All this about me 'having a nice little rest while she got on with her work' was total lies. What she does during my afternoon nap – and presumably what she's done every afternoon since she started working here – is to sit down on the sofa and watch Australian soaps.

She had the nerve this afternoon to try and get me to watch them with her. Huh. I gave the first one a couple of minutes, but oh dear, oh dear . . . Eighteen months of deviousness have made me quite a good judge of acting and, let me tell you, the performances in those things are seriously bad.

So I bawled and screamed and ensured that she didn't enjoy any of it.

DAY 13

Cut out the afternoon nap again today. This time the Juggernaut picked me up straight away – too afraid of missing any of her precious soap.

I bawled and screamed through the first half, but then quietened down. The acting hasn't improved, but there is a certain inept charm in the way the stories are put together.

DAY 14

In spite of the total failure of her previous attempt, the Juggernaut got the three other children and their Mother's Helps round again this morning for another meeting of the misnamed Parent and Toddler Group.

I managed to hit one of the little toads with the hammer that's designed to bang those brightly coloured plastic rods into the brightly coloured plastic table. That didn't go down too well.

And the cat scratched another one quite severely. You know, I may have said some uncharitable things about that cat in the past, but today for the first time I recognized a kindred spirit.

DAY 16

I hardly slept at all during my mid-morning nap today and, because I was more scratchy and belligerent than usual at lunchtime, the Juggernaut tried to put me down for a sleep afterwards.

I kicked and screamed and made an enormous fuss. How dare she try and stop me from watching my Australian soaps?

DAY 20

I woke up before my parents this morning, and it was really lovely. The sun was streaming in, filtered through summer curtains, and it made dappled, shifting patterns on my duvet cover. Birds trilled outside. I felt rested, snug and warm.

I started to gurgle, to make little cooing sounds. I developed these into a string of babbling sentences, not using real words but sounding as though I was.

I thought how smashing it was being a baby, how warm and protected and loved I was. And I thought of the pleasures of not being an adult – of being able to sleep until you wake up naturally, of not having to worry about money or work or where the next meal is coming from. And I felt a warm, loving compassion for my parents.

Then I remembered who the hell I was and started screaming my head off. I'm damned if I'm going to let them sleep on. It's a point of honour for me to wake them up before their clock radio does.

DAY 24

Saturday. This Toilet Training is really getting to Her. I don't know why, but suddenly She seems even more worried about the whole business.

Probably She's just had the latest bulletin on the progress of Baby Einstein. Yes, no doubt that little creep has already got a degree in Nuclear Physics and climbed Everest without oxygen. Whereas my mother's stuck with a Little Sod who isn't yet fully Toilet Trained!

Maybe I should take pity on her. Next time I want to have a bowel movement – or rather 'do a Poo' – perhaps I should just ask for the potty and use it for the purpose intended.

On the other hand, it's such fun having Her chase me round the house on the off-chance, potty at the ready. Why should I spoil such a highlight of our Quality Time together?

DAY 28

This evening I fell down with a bump on my bottom. Thinking that a development in my linguistic skills might get Her mind off Toilet Training for a moment, I distracted Her with a new word. 'Botty,' I said, and then, in case She hadn't got the point, I repeated, 'Botty!'

And guess what She did . . . ? Yes, She produced the potty.

Honestly! If I'd meant potty, I'd have said potty.

DAY 29

I sometimes feel almost guilty about the way I send Her
up, but She does ask for it. It's just like taking candy
from a baby. (Well, like taking candy from some *other*
baby. I'd like to see anyone try to take candy from *me*!)

Today was a good example of Her gullibility. As ever,
She was going on and on about this Toilet Training
business, so after supper I decided to indulge Her.
'Potty!' I said urgently. 'Potty!'

'Oh, what a good baby,' She cooed. 'Oo's asking for
oo's potty, isn't oo then?' Well, of course I was! 'Just like
oo did yesterday, didn't oo then?'

Oh, not again!

Anyway, my request seemed like the answer to Her
wildest dreams. She scurried away to fetch the potty,
whipped off everything below my waist and looked at me
meaningfully. She pointed to the potty and said, 'There
– oo knows what that's for, doesn't oo then?'

''Es.' I nodded. ''Es, 'es.'

She smiled encouragingly.

'Well, do what oo should do with it then. Go on.'

I nodded again. She nodded back at me ecstatically.

I picked up the potty and put it on my head.

DAY 31

Saturday. Today my resistance finally gave. Partly it was just being sick of fighting, partly it was the expression of pathetic anxiety on Her face. Whatever the reason, after lunch I once again called out, 'Potty! Potty!'

She had it to hand this time and within seconds I was stripped to the waist – from the floor upwards, that is – and poised astride the potty.

'Now is oo going to sit down and do a nice Poo?' She cajoled winsomely.

With a sigh, I lowered my buttocks on to the cold plastic.

'Now do a big Poo for Mummy. Big Poo for Mummy. Come on . . .'

The yearning in her face was so pitiful, I strained, did a couple of grunts and – plop, plop – deposited two perfect turds into the bowl.

Good heavens! You'd have thought She'd just been released after five years as a hostage and won the pools on the same day. While I modestly rose to my feet, She snatched the potty from beneath me and gazed down as if at the Crown Jewels.

'Oh, what a clever baby! Look what oo's done for oo's Mummy! What a clever, grown-up baby! Oh, thank oo, says Mummy! Thank oo very much!'

Bearing the potty before Her as if carrying it on a tasselled cushion, She led me upstairs to the bathroom.

'*Now* does oo know what we do?' She chortled. 'We cleans oo's botty, but first . . .' She stopped by the lavatory. 'We do *this*.'

Suddenly She upturned the potty, dropped my precious turds into the bowl and flushed them away.

Huh. Last time I give Her a present.

Twentieth Month

DAY 2

A good example today of conflict between Her and the Juggernaut. It was about the dreaded Toilet Training, and was more proof that you can't have job-sharing on a major project of such importance. My mother was the one who started the process and She jolly well ought to see it through.

I have now got to the stage where She reckons I have made the connection between 'the bodily sensations and the product'. I can tell when I'm about to do a Pee or a Poo and, if I feel like it, am quite capable of calling for the potty and using it in time to avoid an 'accident'.

The significant point is that 'when I feel like it'.

Today is Monday and She, flushed with what She

saw as Her lavatorial success over the weekend, told the Juggernaut all about it.

'Baby'll now call for the potty when it's needed,' She announced confidently. 'But you have to be quick. Be sure you listen out for that cry of "potty!", won't you?'

So was one single cry of 'potty!' heard throughout the entire day? What do you think?

And when She came back from work, was a single cry of 'potty!' heard during the evening? No.

It worked. A little splinter of guilt insinuated itself into Her mind. 'You know,' I heard Her say to Him, 'I do worry about the Mother's Help. In some ways I think she could be holding up Baby's development.'

DAY 3

While the Juggernaut was here today, every time I felt the urge, I yelled 'potty!' at the top of my voice. She always got there in time. There was not a single accident.

It was a day of perfect Toilet Training, as the Juggernaut proudly told Her when She got home from work.

But was a single cry of potty heard during the evening? Be serious.

'You know,' I heard Her say to Him, 'I do worry about the Mother's Help. I think she sometimes tells dreadful lies.'

Stir, stir. Oh, I'm enjoying this!

DAY 4

Another accident-free day and an evening of total incontinence.

Again the Juggernaut reported her success. My mother became even more suspicious of the girl's truthfulness.

DAY 5

Change of tactics today. While the Juggernaut was here, I didn't call for the potty once, but produced three nappies that each looked like a month in the trenches.

After the Juggernaut had reported the setback and gone home, I became suddenly exemplary, asking for the potty twice in ringing tones and doing my impression of the perfectly Toilet-Trained infant.

She is now convinced that the Juggernaut is lying.

DAY 6

When the Juggernaut arrived, She told her about my perfect behaviour of the night before. After She'd gone to work and we were alone together, I regressed to First-Month-style incontinence.

The Juggernaut is now convinced that She is lying.

This is a game I can go on playing for a long time. And it needn't just be about Toilet Training. The variations are infinite. Isn't life fun!

DAY 14

I could have told Her – in fact I did my best to tell Her at the time – that this going-back-to-work nonsense would be more trouble than it was worth – but would She listen?

All it means is that She has less time for everything and fails to enjoy anything because of the huge burden of guilt She feels every waking minute.

And do I do my bit to reduce that feeling of guilt? I assume you're joking.

Let's examine why She went back to work. When He and She were discussing the subject, the reasons they came up with were more or less as follows:

1. To bring in some money.
2. To stimulate Her mind and stop Her vegetating.
3. To help Her and me grow apart, as all parents and children naturally must in time.
4. To have the Mother's Help on hand to share some of the drudgery of child-rearing. (Drudgery? Me?)
5. To give Her back Her own identity, to make Her feel She is more than just my mum. (I really blame the self-help books for this one.)

But this is what really happened:

1. Nearly all the money She brings in goes on paying the Juggernaut, buying extra things for me to compensate for the guilt She feels about having left me and taking more holidays because She's so knackered by working all day and running the house the rest of the time.
2. She's so brain-dead from exhaustion these days

that She hardly has a mind; and She'd give Her right arm for ten minutes' uninterrupted vegetating.

3. I know all parents and children must eventually grow apart, but *I'll* be the one who chooses when that moment happens, thank you very much.

4. In practice, this just doesn't work at all. The Juggernaut lies around on the sofa half the day watching TV and stuffing her face. (Now I know why she's built like a supertanker.) And, as you know, the fact that there are two of them involved just makes it all the easier for me to play one off against the other (SEE THIS MONTH'S ENTRIES ON TOILET TRAINING).

5. She hasn't got Her own identity. She *is* just my mum.

DAY 21

Saturday. A good new wheeze today. Because I am now sufficiently mobile to walk for quite long stretches, She tends not to strap me into my buggy all the time. I climb out when I want to walk and then climb back in when I feel tired. She is very proud of this new ability and says it shows how independent I'm becoming.

Today She took me for a big shop. Because He was off somewhere we couldn't use the car. I walked most of the way there, so on the way back I got into the buggy.

She hung Her loaded shopping baskets on to the buggy handles and started pushing me home. I'm getting quite heavy now, so with the shopping too, She was finding it hard going.

She stopped to sit on a bench for a breather. This was my moment. I climbed out of the buggy, and exactly what I'd anticipated happened. Without my counterweight, the buggy tipped over and Her shopping crashed to the ground.

> **CASUALTIES:** **All but two of a box of a dozen eggs, and, even better, His bottle of whisky – again.**

I'll definitely have another go at this.

DAY 23

Decided I've been too amenable about food recently. Refused to eat anything today except crisps and satsuma segments. When the Juggernaut reported this to my mother, She was gratifyingly anxious.

It's great. Any change in my eating habits still gets Her going.

DAY 24

Stuck to crisps and satsumas at lunchtime. When She got home my mother spent ages preparing other tempting little snacks for me. I wouldn't touch any of them. Eventually She succumbed and gave me crisps and satsumas.

DAY 25

Kept to my new diet. It's driving Her crazy. Beginning to wish I'd chosen chocolate pudding and bananas. I'm getting a bit bored with crisps and satsumas.

DAY 26

A great achievement. She is now so distraught about my eating that She didn't go into work this morning, but took me to the doctor instead.

She announced dramatically that for the last three days I have eaten nothing but crisps and satsumas.

I waited with bated breath. What treatment would the doctor offer? Had to be tests at least, didn't it? Hospital overnight for observation?

But no. The doctor just said, 'Well, they're probably all your baby wants to eat at the moment. Now, if you'll excuse me, I do have sick people to see.'

It's amazing how uncaring doctors are these days.

DAY 27

Forced myself to eat crisps and satsumas today, but I don't think I'll carry on. I mean, if a food fad doesn't worry anyone, there's not much point in it, is there? And anyway, I've got a new craving for fish fingers and Marmite.

DAY 28

Honestly! She is such a victim of advertising. She has only to see a product on telly once and She immediately wants to buy it.

There was an ad on tonight that really got her excited, because it was for something connected with the sacred Toilet Training. Only the lateness of the hour stopped Her rushing straight down to the shops.

Training Pants, that's what the product was. Sort of halfway house between a nappy and a pair of knickers. The gimmick is that the baby is allowed to feel very mature because the Training Pants can be PULLED UP AND DOWN. Wow!

Well, the company which manufactures these things has clearly got the purchasing psychology of parents sussed, but they don't have a clue about what makes babies tick.

A) A baby of my age doesn't frankly get that excited about the idea of wearing knickers, and

B) Any baby worth its salt is going to take advantage of the unique PULLING UP AND DOWN feature to ensure that the Training Pants are DOWN whenever an 'accident' happens, first making sure that they are sitting on their parents' best upholstery.

DAY 29

Guess what! Today She went out and bought some Training Pants.

So next time my nappy was changed I got the full, 'Oo's such a big grown-up baby now that oo's not going

to wear a nappy any more. Look –' She held up a pair of the Training Pants '– oo's got grown-up knickers just like Mummy and Daddy wear.'

Does She really believe that I'm going to confuse a pair of adult briefs with an elasticated paper quilt?

Anyway, She stood me up and pulled the Training Pants up on me. Once She'd got them up, She pulled them down again. Up they went. Down. 'Up, down, up, down, up, down – nice and easy – just like grown-ups do it.'

Eventually She tired of the yo-yo routine and, patting me on the bottom, said, 'There. So now when oo next wants to do a Pee or a Poo, oo just pulls oo's Training Pants down and finds the potty . . . doesn't oo then?'

Well, I did half of what She asked. When I next wanted to do a Pee or a Poo, I pulled my Training Pants down. But I didn't find the potty. Instead I found that nice warm bit by the radiator behind the sofa.

And for good measure I made it a Poo.

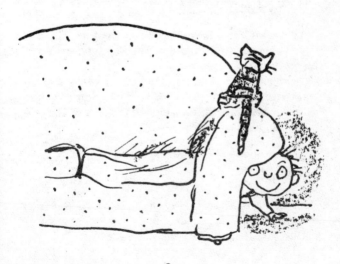

Twenty-First Month

DAY 1

Got given a new toy today. A little red plastic telephone with numbered buttons to press. 'There,' She said. 'Now oo can phone up all oo's friends – just like Mummy and Daddy.'

What does She take me for? I can see it hasn't got any wires attached. And there's no dialling tone when I lift the receiver.

Overheard Her talking to Him this evening about my toy telephone. She used that fatal word again – Educational. And She imagines I'll go near the thing after that. As if.

DAY 2

'Has oo been talking to oo's friends on the telephone then?' She asked me this evening. 'I wish oo would.'

All right. If that's what She wants, I will.

DAY 3

Soon after She'd gone off to work and while the Juggernaut was busy feeding the washing machine my daily half ton of stained clothes, I decided to obey Her wishes and ring one of my friends on the telephone.

Not my tatty red plastic telephone, of course. Oh no, I used theirs. I've watched them using it often enough. All you have to do is pick up the receiver and press a few buttons.

Took quite a few tries before I got anything. Most sequences of numbers I pressed just ended in a whiny sound.

Eventually, though, I got a good one. A voice at the other end answered. I think it was speaking English. I tried out my repertory of words to start a conversation,

but the voice didn't respond. I soon got bored because the sentences just seemed to repeat themselves. So I left the receiver off the hook and went away to try out my new face paints on the cat.

When my mum came back from work, She asked the Juggernaut if there was anything wrong with the phone.

She'd tried ringing a few times from the office, but kept getting an engaged signal.

She then noticed the phone was off the hook, picked up the receiver and listened. Honestly, the fuss She made! Shouting and sobbing, screaming at the Juggernaut that I must never be allowed to go near the phone. And then when He came home, the whole routine started up again and She kept going on about how they wouldn't be able to afford a holiday this year.

No praise for my achievement, mind. Frankly, I think it's quite clever for someone of my age to get through to the Australian Speaking Clock.

G'DAY... ON THE THIRD STROKE...

DAY 8

This morning I totted up all the words I can say.

I started last Christmas Day with a rather unusual First Word – 'cue'. This was a reference to a billiard cue that He had just been given as a present, but which they persisted in thinking was my form of 'Thank you'.

I can actually say 'Thank you' now. Mind you, I don't very often.

Then I got 'No!' on board pretty quickly, and 'More!' came not long after. I can do 'Mum', and if I feel particularly charitable I'll do the odd 'Dad' too. And, until I can master 'Juggernaut', she'll always be 'Bum' to me.

I can do ''es', though unfortunately I can't manage the 'y' sound at the beginning. Still, I don't need it very often. I find 'No!' fits most situations much better.

I can also do 'botty' and 'potty' – though my parents still think the last two are the same word. Then there's 'want', 'pretty', 'cat', 'me', 'bye bye' and 'naughty'.

So how many's that . . . ? Sixteen. About average for twenty-one months, I should think.

DAY 13

It's not just individual words I can say. When the mood takes me, I can combine them into mini-phrases or sentences: 'Want Mum!', 'more potty', that kind of thing.

I haven't yet tried putting them all together into one big sentence. Now how would that work out? Let me think . . .

Yes, it'd be something like:

''Es, Mum, cue Dad, no more naughty botty bum, me want pretty potty, thank you, bye bye cat.'

Mm . . . I may have to wait a while before the right conversational opening comes up.

DAY 16

I am now completely addicted to Children's Television. At first I thought it was a load of rubbish. It still is, but now it's a load of rubbish that I'm hooked on. If I miss my regular fix, there's hell to pay for the rest of the day.

My mother is always telling Her friends that She 'rations' my television viewing, and that She is 'discriminating' about what I'm allowed to watch. This is absolute cobblers. She doesn't give a damn what's on the screen as long as she gets half an hour's peace and quiet out of it.

If television does rot the mind, it's the parents who're responsible for building the compost heap.

DAY 17

I can now turn the television on and off, and change channel, but not in a very controlled way. That is, I can change it, but I don't have a lot of influence over what

I change it to. I am also pretty good with the remote control.

I have three favourite tricks with the remote. One is to take the batteries out and put them somewhere safe like the washing machine. Simple, but effective. Sends them up the wall.

My second trick is to hide it. This drives them to distraction. I've tried all kinds of hiding places. Under the scrotty old blanket in the cat's basket was quite good, but my favourite must be the sandpit.

(Incidentally – and this is an important point – when hiding the remote control, if possible choose somewhere dirty, so that when your parents do finally find the thing there's gunk all over it. And, remember, whenever you're handling it, make sure that you've just been eating something sticky.)

My third good trick with the remote is changing channels at pivotal moments when He's watching sport. You'd be amazed at the fury generated by a well-timed switch across when a long putt is approaching the hole, or when a striker has just received a pass in the area with only the keeper to beat.

DAY 19

Sunday. I am now able to get out of my cot, go downstairs and switch on the television all by myself. They seem terribly keen that I should do this every Sunday morning, though most of my other demonstrations of independence have been greeted with little enthusiasm.

I've taken a while to figure out why, but this morning it came to me in a blinding flash.

They want me out of the way on Sunday mornings so they can have a lie-in. Idle layabouts! Worse than that – they want to have a lie-in so they can indulge in sex. Disgusting!

The minute I realized this, I snuck upstairs and crept quietly into their bedroom. You should have seen the speed with which they sprang apart when they saw me . . .

DAY 21

I got a new word today. When She came back from work, She was getting me a drink in my sucky cup. 'Now what does oo want then?' She cooed. 'Orange or lemon?'

I replied, 'Lenom.'

I wonder why She laughed.

DAY 27

He came back from work this evening and as usual first thing He did was to pour Himself a large whisky. I reached out winsomely to His glass. 'Me! Me!' I pleaded, knowing how much they enjoy these pathetic little charades.

'Oh, look, Baby wants some whisky too,' He chortled. (Honestly, it's so easy to amuse them.)

She decided to play the game through and picked another whisky glass off the shelf. 'Me get whisky for oo,' She announced gravely.

She came back with the glass full of lemon squash and held it out to me. I reached forward to take it, but She didn't let go. Wasn't going to risk a real glass in the hands of someone used to a plastic sucky cup.

I looked at Him. He took a long swig from His glass and smacked His lips with satisfaction.

I played along. Took a long swig from my glass and smacked my lips with satisfaction.

They fell about. Apparently this was the funniest thing they'd ever seen in their poor, humour-starved lives.

'And what is oo drinking then?' She asked.

I decided the frivolity had gone far enough, so in my most sober voice I enunciated, 'Lenom.'

They thought this was, if anything, even funnier.

God knows what they did for fun before I came along.

DAY 28

The Juggernaut was getting me a drink today. She indicated the bottles of orange and lemon squash. 'Which do you want?'

'Lenom,' I replied firmly.

She fell about, just like they had. What is it about the word 'lenom' that makes it such an unfailing rib-tickler?

'No,' she said. 'The word's "lemon". Have you got that?'

'"Lemon",' I said.

'That's right.'

When my mum got home from work, I gave Her a very frosty look. The Juggernaut told Her about our exchange. 'But don't worry, Baby's got it right now,' she concluded.

'Oh, really?' There was a note of disappointment in Her voice. 'I *liked* it when oo said "lenom".'

If I turn out illiterate, there'll be no question about who's to blame.

Twenty-Second Month

DAY 4

Woke up about six. Lay there gurgling and burbling winsomely, considering the options for the morning's excursion.

Now I'm not locked into my cot, I can go anywhere. Where should it be today? Down to the kitchen to open the fridge and spill yoghurt over the floor? Into the sitting room to stuff Wagon Wheels into the CD player?

Decided instead to go into their bedroom. They were fast asleep – with the cat lying on the duvet between them. Huh. The fuss they make about me coming into their bed and yet that mangy beast is allowed to stay with them *all* night.

Saw off the cat with a practised and extremely painful tail-tweak. Heard the cat-flap slam as I climbed into my parents' bed. Managed to wriggle in between them. Nice and warm it was.

DAY 5

Woke at three in the morning. Was about to scream for comfort and rescue when I suddenly realized I didn't need to. Got out of my cot and joined them in their bed. This could become a habit.

DAY 6

They are getting very sick of my new independence, which is disrupting their sleep patterns in a most gratifying way. It is remarkable how much space in a bed a determined toddler can take up.

In fact my experimentation in this area has led me to produce the following set of statistics:

	Percentage over Body Area of Bed Space Taken Up	Percentage of Duvet Appropriated
NORMAL ADULT	17%	50%
CAT	56%	37%
LITTLE SOD	184%	100%

DAY 7

'There's no point in fighting it,' She said to Him this morning. (It's always very heartwarming for me when She starts a conversation like that.) 'Baby's outgrown the cot. Time for the transfer to a bed, I think. Baby'll really like being in a grown-up bed. And it'll stop this constant coming into our bed in the mornings.'

Well, She was fifty per cent right.

DAY 11

Suddenly struck me this morning that I haven't been ill for a while, so I concentrated hard and came up with a really quite presentable rash on my chest and arms.

It was certainly spectacular enough for Her to have all the childcare books laid out over the sitting room floor this evening while She tried to match up my rash with the illustrations.

She concluded that it's not mottled enough for German measles and not eruptive enough for chickenpox. Now she's really worried. Thinks I might have an illness hitherto unknown to medical science.

DAY 12

To my disappointment, when I woke up this morning, my unidentifiable rash had completely vanished.

So I decided to have a cold instead. I mean, obviously I've had them before – little, snuffly numbers – but not a really big, major one.

I'm glad I saved it up till I was properly mobile. It's easy for a parent to swoop down and wipe the nose of an unmoving baby, but much more difficult when the child can scurry about looking for new surfaces on which to deposit snot.

I began it during the day while the Juggernaut was here. Just a minor runny nose to start with, dribbling down into my mouth, which I held slightly open, so that snot and saliva could mingle and then dribble down my chin on to my clothes. The Juggernaut caught on to this with distressing speed and very quickly put a towelling bib round my neck, which was extremely frustrating.

'Bit snuffly,' she announced whem my mum came home from work. 'Been a bit snuffly all day.'

'But nothing serious?' She asked with that knee-jerk anxiety which the state of my health always inspires in Her. 'The rash hasn't come back?'

'No, it's just a cold,' said the Juggernaut, putting on her new fur-collared coat as she prepared to leave.

This was the moment for one of my spontaneous outbursts of lovability. Given my relationship with the Juggernaut, she was more than a bit surprised when I launched myself at her and started smothering her face and neck with big slobbery kisses. I must say, the snot matted into the fur of her collar very satisfactorily.

When she had managed to make good her escape, I turned the focus of my affection on to my mother. She was wearing a new black business suit which, I'm proud to say, looked like a Grand Prix circuit for snails by the time I'd finished with it.

She was torn. Fury about Her new suit was tempered with sympathy for me feeling ill and gratitude for how brave I was being about it. So She controlled Her anger and went to get my supper.

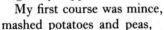

My first course was mince, mashed potatoes and peas, followed by pureed apple and yoghurt. The good thing about both these dishes is that, from the visual point of view, once they're all mushed up they're almost indistinguishable from snot.

So everything that trickled from my nose and everything that trickled from my mouth formed a wonderful goo which I managed to get all over my clothes, my high chair and my mother whenever She came close enough.

She then bathed me and I slimed up the towels pretty thoroughly too. By this stage I decided I'd done enough being brave about the whole business, and started to grizzle.

I'm quite good at grizzling. The skill is to home in on one infuriating note and keep coming back to it. I was a real pain and kept grabbing at Her front in hopes that She'd let me regress to a quick slurp, but She resisted that. The thought of snot all over Her breasts was more than She could cope with.

When She put me down in my bed, I maintained the grizzle and brought in a refinement – a sudden snort in the middle of all the sniffles, as if my passages were so blocked up I couldn't breathe.

That really got Her worried, and I'm confident that She had one of those nights when She hardly dared doze off at all in case I choked.

I slept like a top.

DAY 13

Woke up with my sleeping suit, sheet and duvet drenched in snot. Went through and climbed into their bed, so that I could cover their sheet, duvet, nightwear and bodies with more snot.

All day my nose went on pouring the stuff out like a cement mixer.

I also perfected a new trick – letting a long tendril descend from my nostrils and then, just before it broke off, moving my head suddenly sideways so that it swung across rather like a whiplash. I got more accurate with this during the day, and by the time my mother got back from the office, I could land a glob on the Juggernaut's jeans from two metres. Not bad, huh?

Incidentally, when She did come home, my mum was carrying a plastic-covered package on a hanger. She'd clearly been to the dry cleaner's with Her new black suit. I eyed it hungrily, longing for a bit of snot-splashing practice with that as a target.

The Juggernaut left very quickly before I could give her another spontaneous demonstration of physical affection. She said she wanted to get home as soon as possible because she was feeling a bit off colour.

My mother did the feeding, bathing, putting to bed routine and then spoke to me very seriously. 'Look, I've got an important meeting tomorrow and I must work hard preparing for it this evening . . . so you will be a good baby and just settle down with no fuss, won't you?'

You'd have thought She'd had me around long enough by now not to tempt fate with fatuous questions like that.

DAY 14

I slept pretty well, but was woken early by the sounds of Her getting out of bed. She was trying to catch up on the preparation for Her meeting that I had prevented Her from doing the night before.

I had no alternative but to go into my full groaning, snuffling and apparently-stopping-breathing routine. So She didn't get any work done in the morning, either.

He, who is sometimes no fool, had to rush off to the office early. He scurried out wishing Her lots of luck for the big meeting, and so wasn't there to witness Her, in Her cleaned black suit, angrily pacing up and down waiting for the Juggernaut to arrive.

Nor was He there to hear the phonecall from the Juggernaut saying that she'd caught my cold and wouldn't be able to come in today.

He didn't hear my mother's scream of fury, either. Or Her crawling phonecall to Her boss to apologize for not being able to make the meeting.

Nor did He see, until the evening, Her black suit, over which I'd smeared so much snot it looked like an accident in a glue factory.

DAY 15

I felt better this morning. In fact, I haven't really felt bad at all with this cold. Not that I was going to let them know that.

No. I kept up the full grizzling and whining routine. The supplies of snot are beginning to dry up, but I supplemented them as far as possible with saliva and mushed-up banana.

The Juggernaut was still ill. Apparently with her my cold's turned into a rather nasty bout of flu. So She had to stay at home again. There were a few angry calls from the office, and She kept saying that this was exceptional,

She was perfectly capable of holding down a demanding job and She wasn't at Her baby's beck and call every minute of the day. She lives in a dreamworld.

By my bathtime She was looking pretty grisly and, as soon as He came back from work, She retired to bed saying She was aching all over.

He was in charge, and so it was He who had to deal with all my snuffling and grizzling through the night. I made the most of it.

DAY 18

She is totally prostrated by flu. The Juggernaut's still laid up with it, so He had to stay at home and look after me.

He rang work to tell them and got quite an earful from His boss, who clearly is of the old school and has never encountered the concept of a New Man.

I was snuffly and grizzly and as snotty as I could manage. By the end of the day, He was

A) exhausted, and

B) starting to feel rather achy.

Ever generous in triumph, I decided not to give them too bad a night.

DAY 20

He's now totally prostrated by flu. So that's all three of them down.

Her mother was brought in to look after me. My supplies of snot have now completely dried up, but I still managed to be very snuffly and clinging.

He complained that Her mother spoils me. This is entirely true, and I'm even more of a pain than usual after she's been round.

Her mother complained that He was making a big fuss about being ill, and that men always are bad invalids.

By the end of the day Her mother was feeling very achy.

DAY 21

Her mother couldn't come back today to look after me because she's got the flu. So's He. So's She. And the Juggernaut rang in to say she's still got it too.

As a result, His mother came to look after me.

She complained that His mother spoils me. This is entirely true, etc.

His mother complained that my mother didn't show much sympathy for Him when He was ill. He'd always been delicate. Also His mother wasn't very impressed with my mother's standards of cleanliness in the kitchen.

By the end of the day His mother was feeling very achy.

DAY 22

His mother couldn't come back today to look after me because she's got the flu. So's He. So's She.

The Juggernaut, however, was feeling a bit better, so she came in. She was pretty groggy again by the end of the day.

Me, I feel fine. I have all through.

But, you know, I think I can feel another cold coming on any day now.

Twenty-Third Month

DAYS 12–14

Fat lot of Quality Time I got this weekend. My parents had the nerve to go away to a hotel for what they coyly referred to as 'a second honeymoon'. And if that wasn't bad enough, they dumped me on Her mother for the duration.

'Don't worry about a thing,' the old girl said when I was handed over. 'I'm sure Baby won't give me any trouble at all.'

I can now see where my mother gets Her gullibility from.

DAY 15

Her mother booked into a health farm for a fortnight to get over the weekend.

DAY 20

Saturday. My mobility skills are now very well developed. I can choose the direction in which I move; forward, reverse, sideways. I can do a three-point turn. I can control my speed, accelerating and slowing down with smooth efficiency. I can do an emergency stop.

This does not mean that I deploy all these skills to the full. Oh no. I am a toddler, and so it's a point of honour for me to toddle.

And toddling, properly practised, can be one of the most infuriating experiences in the world to a toddler's adult companion. Like all the best parent-aggravating ploys, it prompts two conflicting reactions. My mother and father are torn between admiration for my skills, together with a willingness to encourage my development – and blind fury at the sheer slowness of my progress.

Let us take today as an example. And, incidentally, any fellow Little Sods reading this could do a lot worse than take it as a template for perfect ITT (Irritating Toddler Technique).

The skilled practitioner of ITT will be greatly helped by the use of a few simple phrases. 'Me do it!' is an important one, but 'Me look!' and 'Pretty!' can come in handy as well. 'Carry!' is also essential, and should always be accompanied by an imperious upstretched arm gesture, together with that trembling bottom lip which presages tears.

And, as in all dealings with parents, never fail to be armed with that most important of words – 'No!'

Today being a Saturday both parents very firmly set out to give me Quality Time – whether I wanted it or not. 'We'll go to the shops,' She said, 'and then after that we'll go and feed the ducks – oo'd like that, wouldn't oo then?'

I decided it was too early for my first 'No!' of the day, so instead I said, ''Ucks, 'ucks.' Obviously I'm perfectly capable of saying 'ducks' if I want to, but my parents seem to get such a charge out of my pronouncing words wrong that it would be churlish to disappoint them.

Because it was cold, this morning's expedition started by getting me dressed in sufficient layers: jumpers, zip-up waterproof jacket, scarves, gloves, etc. Because I am sometimes capable of getting a few garments on by myself, this proved an opportunity for a lot of 'Me do it!' and all those well-loved routines of putting arms through neck-holes, heads through sleeves, etc.

This is a wonderful example of ITT, which can be extended almost indefinitely. Parents are so keen on the idea of their toddlers dressing themselves that they will undergo agonies of tedium watching their offspring's ineptitude before their nerve finally cracks.

His went first (never a big surprise at the weekends). 'Look, are we going out or aren't we?' he snapped pettishly.

'We're going out just as soon as Baby's dressed,' She countered.

'Well, why don't you bloody dress Baby then?'

'Because Baby's doing it for Baby's self.'

'Oh, for God's sake!'

By then most of my clothes were on. She leant forward to do up the zip of my jacket. I turned away with another 'Me do it!'

This was too much even for Her. She's spent too many hours of Her life watching me fiddle aimlessly with zips. 'No!' She snarled. '*Me* do it!'

For a moment I contemplated the full Temper Tantrum reaction to this, but decided against it. The whole point of this exercise – and a useful general rule for students of ITT – was that I should appear to be TRYING TO HELP.

Eventually we managed to get out of the house and into the car. As soon as I was put in the car seat, I reached ineptly for the straps and once again announced, 'Me do it!'

'No, if we wait for that, we'll be here all bloody morning!' He snapped, and incarcerated me in the seat as if he were trussing a turkey.

The place where they shop on Saturdays is one of those big pedestrian precincts with rows of shops on either side. Because there are so many people about, these are absolutely perfect arenas for ITT.

I won't detail my precise movements this morning, but here's an outline of the sort of ploys which I have found in the past to be most effective.

BASIC TODDLING MOVEMENT

It is best to start at the parent's side. Try to avoid having your hand held, as this may restrict your range. A confident, 'Me do it!' will often get the hand released, as the parent is impressed by your independence and, having read the appropriate childcare books, realizes that too much restraint may stunt your psychological development.

Once you're in motion, move gradually across your parent's line of advance, while gently but steadily decelerating. This means that your parent has to take evasive action to avoid tripping over you.

This is where that emergency stop you've practised comes in. Don't use it all the time, vary your technique, but every now and then coming to a complete halt right in front of your parent's legs can be absolutely devastating.

A few repetitions of this basic manoeuvre are guaranteed to reduce your parent to a gibbering wreck within five minutes.

But remember, at all times be amiable. Lots of plucky smiles and little grins of triumph at how well you're doing cannot fail to add to your parent's anger and guilt.

LINGERING TECHNIQUE

Toddling behind is at least as effective as cutting up from the front. Start at a grown-up pace, but gradually get slower and slower. It is remarkable how quickly you can drop a very long way behind an adult in a hurry.

Don't stop altogether, otherwise you're likely to be picked up and whisked away, or put back into your buggy. Just move infinitely slowly, with a fixed smile of noble endeavour on your face. Remember to burst into tears if your parents are driven to shout at you, particularly if there are any little old ladies present.

DARTING OFF

Especially effective in crowds, this technique, which can be accomplished either from in front of or behind, is guaranteed to engender panic in even the most placid of parents.

It is important that the angle of your dart veers off the course that your parent is currently following. The initial movement should be very fast, so that you're out of sight before anyone is aware of your absence. Then you can slow down, or even stop.

A good wrinkle for darting off is, when you're out of sight, to stop in front of something and behave as if it's the most fascinating object you've ever encountered in your entire life. Then, when your hysterical parent finally finds you, you point winsomely at the fluffy pink hippopotamus in the shop window (or whatever) and say, 'Pretty!'

At such moments parents find it difficult to cope with their conflicting emotions.

TODDLING WITH BUGGY

Everything that applies to basic toddling skills can be made even more destructive if you're armed with a buggy.

As soon as you've been lifted out of the buggy and told to walk, indicate that you want to push it. You will probably encounter opposition at this point, but insist on your rights. It may even be worth indulging in a small Temper Tantrum.

Once you have wrested the buggy from your parent, just follow the manoeuvres detailed above. Since the movements of a buggy even under the control of a responsible adult are as erratic as those of a supermarket trolley, in your hands it becomes a major traffic hazard.

A TIP: When manoeuvring your buggy through crowds, for maximum impact be sure to target other toddlers, pets and the old and infirm.

Never forget the buggy's basic instability. When you need to stop or stage an accident or simply engage sympathy, just sit down while keeping firm hold of the handles, and the buggy will tip up.

This is particularly satisfying if your mother has piled her shopping up in the buggy, as it will almost definitely spill out.

RESTRAINING DEVICES

These are barbaric inventions of the Devil which ensure that parent and toddler are actually physically joined. They may take the form of old-fashioned reins, or of those handcuff-like devices with what looks like curled telephone wire joining them.

Try to avoid such equipment if possible. The first time you are put into your bonds, twist, turn, scream and generally make as much of a nuisance of yourself as you can. If all else fails, try wriggling and squirming until the straps become twisted round your neck. (Parents always react quickly to things you manage to twist round your neck.)

In the unhappy event of all such efforts failing, do not despair. There are techniques available which can make a virtue even of these inhuman devices.

Remember the old Little Sod maxim:

Straps and strings
Can get tangled up in things.

So aim to get as far away from your parent as possible and maximize the restraint's potential. Because you are quite near the ground, a taut string acts as a wonderful trip-wire. Again target other toddlers, pets and – particularly – anyone over the age of sixty.

If there are none of these in evidence, there will always be trees, litter bins, post boxes, lamp-posts, etc. Just use your imagination.

GETTING OUT OF TODDLING MODE

When you've exhausted the destructive possibilities of toddling, or when you're just exhausted, the way out is simple.

Stop dead, raise your arms and shout, 'Carry!'

Resist all attempts to make you move any further.

Incidentally, make sure you use this ploy at just the right moment. Wait till your mother's arms are full of shopping, or till you've reached the bottom of the hill that has to be climbed up again to get you home.

If you've got the buggy with you, of course the 'Carry!' ploy is not going to work. In this case, resort to the basic Starfish Position (as detailed in *How to be a Little Sod*, p. 91), arms and legs outstretched, so that it takes ages to get you strapped into the buggy. Once in it, follow all the usual slipping-down, throwing-off-gloves, trailing-hand-in-the-dirt, grabbing-hold-of-passing-objects routines, which should be second nature to you by now.

GENERAL POINTS ON TODDLING

In the above the word 'parent' has been used throughout, but all techniques described are just as effective in the company of a Mother's Help, nanny, grandparent, etc.

And they're all at their most effective in supermarkets.

Anyway, I did the lot this morning and, by the end of the shopping my parents were so frazzled that we gave feeding the ducks a miss. Didn't bother me. So far as I'm concerned, you've seen one duck you've seen them all.

Mind you, that didn't stop me grizzling throughout the rest of the day, reproachfully murmuring, ''Ucks. 'Ucks.'

'ELLO 'UCKS

Twenty-Fourth Month

DAY 1

I am so sick of my parents continually trying to get me to 'make friends' with other revolting, snotty little kids that I've decided to invent a friend of my own.

'Dirpy'. That's its name – 'Dirpy'. I haven't yet decided whether to make Dirpy a boy or a girl.

DAY 4

Saturday. Decided that today would be the day to introduce Dirpy to the waiting world. Or at least to Her.

I planned Dirpy's first appearance with great care. She was making another of Her pathetic attempts with the Training Pants, so I chose my moment to do a Pee in the kitchen.

QUICK DIGRESSION ON THE BEST PLACES TO PEE

The decision is really down to you, but you have to weigh up the effect you are trying to create. Peeing on a shiny surface like a kitchen floor tends to be more instantly noticeable than peeing on a carpet – though that does depend a bit on the colour of the carpet.

The disadvantages of peeing on a shiny floor are:
A) Your pee can be mistaken for some other spillage, and
B) It is very easily mopped up.

The disadvantages of peeing on a carpet are:
A) It doesn't make a nice splashy noise, and
B) In the short term nobody may notice that you have peed there.
But the big advantage of peeing on a carpet is that *in the long term* they do notice. And how!

TIP: Try peeing on the same spot every day for a week.

Choose your target area carefully. It should not be too obvious or your pee will be noticed immediately and cleaned up. Select somewhere out of sight – behind a sofa is ideal. And if you can actually pee near a radiator, even better. Its warmth will considerably enhance the maturity of the resulting aroma.

At the end of about a week you should be rewarded by expressions of distaste and wrinkled noses from every guest who comes to the house. With a bit of luck your parents may well not notice the smell because they've spent more time there and it's sort of crept up on them gradually.

And of course don't forget that anything you can do with Pee can also be done with Poo. Trouble is, parents do tend to notice that quicker – particularly if you're trying to build up a pile of the stuff on the carpet.

Anyway, where was I? Oh yes – Dirpy.

Right, so I'd got the Training Pants down and just peed on the kitchen floor while Her back was turned. She looked round, saw the little pool and said, 'Oh dear. Now oo's done that then?'

'Dirpy,' I said proudly.

'Yes, it is,' She said, '– very dirty.'

I can't bear it! Was ever a child more misunderstood?

DAY 6

All that Christmas business is starting up again. Children's Television is full of it. All these idiotic presenters keep appearing in Santa costumes, and they even stuck a sprig of holly on that toilet roll I'm still meant to believe is a mouse.

The commercials are quite disgusting. They just pander to greed. Clearly it is reckoned to be beneath the dignity of any child to ask for a Christmas present costing less than £49.99.

Hm . . . Maybe I should add 'Sega' and 'Nintendo' to my growing list of words.

DAY 8

This evening, after She came back from work, She got out a piece of paper and some crayons and got me to do a drawing. I don't mind doing this, and will scribble away cheerfully for quite a while. Mind you, the minute I hear Her use the word 'Educational', I stop.

Anyway, when I'd got bored, She picked up my doodle like it was a Dead Sea Scroll and said, 'There.. Hasn't oo written a lovely letter to Santa then?'

What?

She proceeded to throw the paper on to the fire, saying, 'Well, we'll have to see if Santa brings oo any of those uvvy things, won't we then?'

I wonder how long it'll be before She has to be institutionalized?

DAY 11

Since what I want for Christmas seems to have become an issue, I have made a decision. There's this commercial that keeps being on telly for a kind of games console called a 'Super-Mega-CD-Blaster'. It's a snip at £249.99.

I want one of those.

DAY 12

Spent today practising saying 'Super-Mega-CD-Blaster', so that I'll have my answer ready when someone asks me what I want for Christmas.

DAY 18

Saturday. 'Got a big surprise for oo today,' She announced after She'd got me dressed this morning.

I greeted this with my customary scepticism, which increased when it became apparent that all we were doing was going shopping. I mean, as we've done that nearly every Saturday since my birth, I could be forgiven for not rating it particularly high in the surprise stakes.

When we got to the pedestrian precinct, I was keen to do a bit of my toddling routine, cutting up passers-by, felling a few pensioners, etc., but She had other ideas. 'No,' She said, strapping me firmly into the buggy. 'We must hurry if we want to get there before the queue builds up.' And She whisked me off into a big store.

I was taken up in the lift and emerged in the Toy Department. I quite wanted to linger by the toy displays, but wasn't allowed to. Instead I was whizzed along to what looked like a tunnel made of corrugated cardboard covered in tinsel. By a cash register stood a small queue of determined-looking parents and bemused-looking kids. She got me (still buggy-bound) in line behind the others.

I thought this was dead boring and started to grizzle. 'Don't make a fuss,' She cooed. 'Oo's going to have an uvvy surprise.'

Eventually we got to the head of the queue and She paid out what seemed to me – considering She didn't get anything in return – an inordinate amount of money. Then She unstrapped me from the buggy and led me to the opening of the tinsel tunnel. It was awash with fairy lights.

'Now who does oo think oo's going to meet down there?' She asked soppily.

Well, I didn't know, did I?

'Off oo go and find out,' She said, giving me a little push in the back.

I'm an accommodating soul, so off I trudged down the tunnel. She followed a few steps behind.

I turned a corner and was suddenly confronted by a ghastly sight. An evil old man with a white beard and a serious drinker's complexion leered at me from out of a big throne. 'Hello,' he croaked. 'Are you going to come and sit on my knee?'

I did what any self-respecting toddler would have done. I screamed, turned on my heel and belted back down the tunnel.

She blocked my progress with a move an All Black full-back wouldn't have been ashamed of and, forcing me into an arm-lock, said firmly, 'Come on, oo wants to see Santa, doesn't oo then?'

I do despair sometimes. My screams, my body language, everything about me announced with crystal clarity that the last thing on God's earth I wanted to do was go to and see Santa. But that didn't deter Her. I was frogmarched back to the grotto towards this revolting old man, who continued to leer at me through his disgusting foliage of facial hair.

'Now oo's going to sit on Santa's lap, isn't oo then?' She cooed, picking me up to place me on the alien knee.

I kicked out in every direction, and am glad to say one hard little shoe caught Santa through the beard on the tip of his chin. He recoiled and She gave up the idea of putting me on his lap.

'Still, oo'd like to shake Santa's hand, wouldn't oo?' She offered as an alternative. (This is a new trick of mine. I don't particularly like shaking people's hands, but my parents get such childish pleasure out of seeing me do it that I occasionally indulge them.)

Santa, a mask of bonhomie on his florid face, reached out a white-gloved hand towards me. I bit it. Hard. He withdrew his hand sharply.

'What's your name?' he asked with markedly less bonhomie.

I was damned if I was going to tell him. If he knew who I was, he might try to come and get me at my house.

But She betrayed me and gave my name. She also told him where we lived, 'So that you'll be able to come and see Baby on Christmas Eve.'

Was She mad? I started screaming again.

'And what do you want for Christmas?' asked Santa, whose stocks of bonhomie were being depleted at an alarming rate.

This at least was a question I could answer. Loudly and clearly I replied, 'A Super-Mega-CD-Blaster.'

'Oh, well, that's very interesting,' said Santa. He

reached into one of the boxes beside his throne, pulled out a gift-wrapped packet and handed it to me.

My eyes dried instantly. Maybe having to meet strange old men in red suits wasn't so bad, after all. I'd never thought that getting a 'Super-Mega-CD-Blaster' would be as easy as that.

'Say thank you,' She said.

'Thank you,' I said.

The minute we got outside the grotto, I ripped the paper off my present. I couldn't wait to see my Super-Mega-CD-Blaster.

Do you know what I got? A badly painted made-in-Korea toy car that hadn't even got a motor in it. Huh!

DAY 25

Christmas Day. This was so like last year's that it's hardly worth chronicling.

Both sets of grandparents came and were icily polite until after lunch. Then, their tongues loosened by alcohol, they started to say what they really thought of each other.

Presents were exchanged. Imagine my distress when I found that, in spite of my saying the words more or less continuously for the past fortnight, nobody gave me a Super-Mega-CD-Blaster. I showed how hurt I was by ignoring the rest of my presents and getting hopelessly overtired. And, yes, of course – it ended in tears.

Is Christmas Day going to be like this for the rest of my life?

DAY 27

There's been a lot of giggling going on recently between my parents. They're up to something. No doubt, as usual, it's something they shouldn't be up to. I must keep an eye on them.

DAY 29

My mother asked me a fatuous question when She got back from work today. 'What would oo think if oo heard Mummy was going to have another baby?'

My thoughts on the subject were extremely clear. I would think it an appalling idea, and I left them in no doubt as to my feelings. Apart from anything else it would be an act of grotesque irresponsibility. She has only recently returned to work after a long lay-off; to contemplate leaving again so soon would be deeply disloyal to Her boss.

Also, given Her cavalier attitude to my upbringing, I really do not think She is a suitable parent for further children. Her limited stock of maternal instinct is spread thin enough with just me in the house.

DAY 31

I have been betrayed! Oh, the perfidy! The sheer inconsiderate heartlessness of what has happened takes my breath away!

Following my unequivocally clear response yesterday to Her whimsical notion of having another baby, you'll never believe what She had the nerve to do today.

She made sure He was there too, picked me up, put

me on Her knee and said, 'Now, Mummy and Daddy have got a very big exciting surprise for you . . .'

You know my thoughts on their ideas of what constitutes an exciting surprise. I started to pick a fascinating encrustation of snot out of my nose.

'Yes,' He enthused. 'It's really good news.'

Unaware of the bombshell about to hit me, I detached a solid nugget from my nose and put it in my mouth.

'Guess what . . . ?' She giggled coyly. 'No, you tell.'

He giggled too. 'No, you.'

Bored with all this, I chomped on my lump of snot.

'I'm going to have another baby!' She announced.

My mouth dropped open. The half-chomped lump of snot dribbled out on a string of saliva.

'Yes,' He picked up. 'You're going to have a little brother or sister!'

He beamed at me. She beamed at me. 'Well . . .' She said. 'What do you think about that?'

There were many things I could have said, but I restricted myself to the rudest words at my disposal.

'BUM! POO! BOTTY!'

And, while She, as ever getting the wrong end of the stick, rushed off to get the potty, one thought dominated my mind:

THIS MEANS WAR!